Sea Mammals of the World

BERNARD STONEHOUSE

ILLUSTRATED BY MARTIN CAMM

Newly born grey seal

PENGUIN BOOKS

Penguin Books Ltd, Harmondsworth, Middlesex, England
Penguin Viking Inc., 40 West 23rd Street, New York, New York 10010, U.S.A.
Penguin Books Australia Ltd, Ringwood, Victoria, Australia
Penguin Books Canada Ltd, 2801 John Street, Markham, Ontario, Canada L3R 1B4
Penguin Books (N.Z.) Ltd, 182–190 Wairau Road, Auckland 10, New Zealand

First published 1985

Filmset in 8 on 9½ pt Ehrhardt by
Rowland Phototypesetting Ltd,
Bury St Edmunds, Suffolk
Printed in Portugal

Contents

Juvenile Hooded Seal, in the blue natal fur for which the species is hunted

Foreword

This book pays tribute to the mammals that dominate the oceans – the fully maritime seals, whales and sirenians especially, and the Polar Bears and marine otters that live on the edge of the sea.

It is partly a field guide, but mainly an identification book – one that gives identity to the animals in it. Few of its readers may ever meet Fraser's Dolphins, Leopard Seals or West African Manatees, or need to put names to them. If they do, this book is enough of a field guide to help, though that is not its main purpose. But many readers hear of whales and other sea mammals, see films and pictures of them, and learn all too often of one species or another in danger from pollution, over-exploitation or mismanagement. This book should help to give identity – to show what the species look like, to give a little information on their background, numbers and ways of life, and to summarize what is interesting about them.

Artist Martin Camm and I thank the many sea-mammal specialists whose published works we have drawn on; we hope that, in simplifying and condensing, we have not misinterpreted or misrepresented their hard-won information. We both owe a special debt of gratitude to Sidney Brown, of the Sea Mammal Research Unit, Cambridge, for help with illustrations and references.

Bernard Stonehouse

Introduction

Sea mammals of all kinds, and whales and seals in particular, have for long held a special fascination for man. Fish-like in form, and living in a fishy environment, they are clearly so much *more* than fish – more versatile and intellectual, more entertaining – with knowing eyes and warmth that no fish ever aspired to. Primitive man, a lively predator, probably found them more tasty than fish, and their oils and furs a useful bonus. But nearly all sea mammals are predators too, and would no doubt have seen his point of view. Their magic lies partly in a paradox. Most mammals, including ourselves, are highly terrestrial. We evolved from fish-like ancestors but are now well adapted, after aeons of struggle and selection, for life on land. Yet the whales, seals and other sea mammals – all kinfolk of ours – have renounced land. Surrendering their hard-won birthright, climbing *down* the family tree, they have gone back to live in the sea, where they are cheerfully beating the fishes at their own game.

Returning to the sea involves more than a mere reversion; these mammals have developed new adaptations and skills, as well as refurbishing old ones. The primitive land mammals ancestral to us both diverged into stocks that went their separate ways some seventy million years ago. The advanced sea mammals – the whales, seals and sirenians – have taken all of this time to develop their professional approach; beating the fishes is no game for amateurs.

Every mammal can swim; some even enjoy it, but an hour in the water is enough to show any land mammal where the sea mammal's proficiency lies. Whether man, elephant or aardvark, we are the wrong shape for swimming, wrong-limbed, wrongly muscled and balanced, and the wrong density. Without proper propellors, control surfaces or streamlining we cannot slip easily through water, and we can neither breathe properly nor hold our breath long enough to be efficient. We cannot see, hear or smell properly under water, and are liable to choke if we try to eat. The porous, glandular skin that serves us so well in air soon becomes useless in water. It waterlogs and lets out heat far faster than we can replace it; hence the chill that numbs land mammals in any but the warmest seas, and the need for Channel swimmers to be greased and well upholstered with fat. So land mammals that fall into the sea (including humans decked out in wet suits, face masks, air bottles and plastic flippers) come quickly to appreciate an evolutionary truth – sea mammals are well adapted indeed for life in their difficult and demanding medium.

Evolution of sea mammals

How did this adaptation come about? Crowded together on the three tenths of the world called dry land, in fierce competition with each other for food and living space, land mammals find much advantage in living by the sea. Coasts and estuaries are often well stocked with plants and a variety of animal foods, easily accessible for a land mammal that is willing to get wet. This is probably

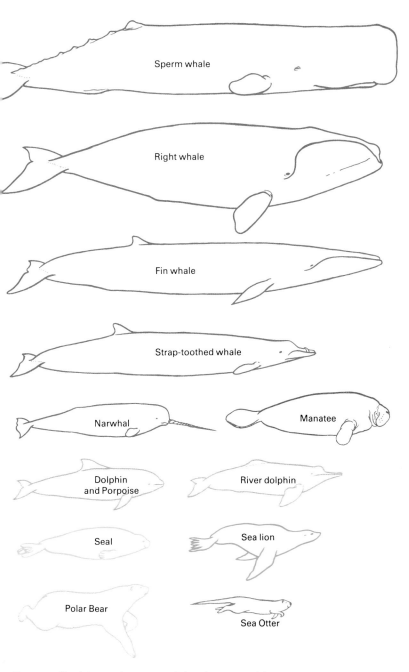

The streamlined shapes of sea mammals (not drawn to scale)

Sperm whale

Right whale

Fin whale

Strap-toothed whale

Narwhal

Manatee

Dolphin and Porpoise

River dolphin

Seal

Sea lion

Polar Bear

Sea Otter

how the ancestors of the modern sea mammals took to marine life. Polar Bears and Sea Otters, the first animals in this book, show how they may have begun. Sea Otters are the maritime branch of a subfamily of carnivorous animals that have long made their living in lakes and streams. Like their freshwater kin, the Sea Otters keep one foot at least on land. They swim and dive well, but can also run, walk and scramble over rocks with their webbed feet, and they come ashore to breed. The fur and subdermal fat that help them to keep warm in cold water equip them also for living in cold climates, where predators and competitors are fewer and shores tend to be richer. Active carnivores with strong teeth and sharp wits, they live close inshore and find most of their food on the sea bed.

There were similar opportunities for coastal living seventy to a hundred million years ago when recognizable ancestors of the modern mammals – both terrestrial and aquatic – were starting to appear. Carnivorous land mammals were already well established and moving into aquatic habitats; among them were the ancestors of the seals, a group that has taken to the sea more fully than Sea Otters. Seals are poorly represented in the fossil record. The earliest known, dating from the early or mid Miocene of about twenty million years ago, show that the families we know today were already extant, with a long semi-aquatic ancestry behind them. The first seals were bear-like, or otter-like, or both (p. 23); while retaining some efficiency on land, their descendants became adept at swimming and diving, with agility enough to catch moving prey in the water.

Modern seals may spend weeks or months continuously at sea, but still return to land – usually once a year – for breeding; they come ashore also to sleep and loaf in the sun. Originating in cool northern climates, they were undismayed when the Ice Age brought intense cold to polar regions; many species live in the world's coldest waters and haul out on to floating ice instead of land. Though more agile in the water than out, they can move fast over snow or sandy beaches; a determined fur seal can outrun a man over cobbles; on the Snares Islands one even out-climbed me on rough rocks, to the surprise of us both.

While the seals were evolving as inshore fishermen, the whales were already established in deeper waters. The earliest known fossil whales (Archaeoceti) date from Lower and Middle Eocene deposits fifty to sixty million years old. Fully aquatic animals, with world-wide distribution, the archaeocetes had long bodies and reduced limbs, with nostrils on top of their skulls like modern whales; they probably sprang from coast-living carnivorous ancestors of the early Eocene or before, and may have passed through an intermediate seal-like stage before heading for the open sea. Archaeocetes disappeared finally some twenty-five million years ago, leaving forerunners of the two remaining groups of whales – Mysticeti and Odontoceti – already recognizable and completely aquatic.

Sirenians, a much smaller order of herbivorous sea mammals, parallel the whales in their fossil history. They share ancestors with the elephants, but were fully aquatic in the Eocene and have changed little over the years. Formerly world-wide, they are now restricted mainly to warm waters. Sailors

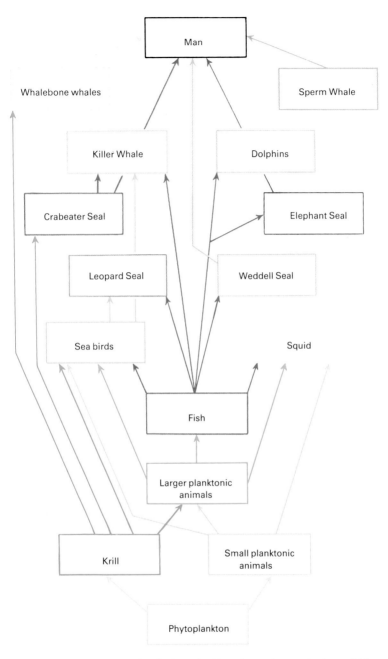

A food web in the sea. All marine life depends ultimately on microscopic plants which 'fix' the sun's energy and make it available for animals

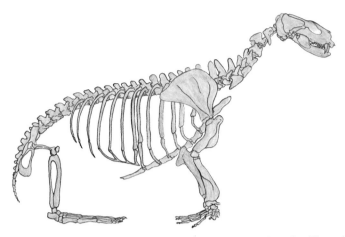

Skeleton of a sea lion; it is similar to that of a land mammal, but has large feet (flippers), relatively massive shoulders and small, very flexible hindquarters

call them sea cows; they include manatees and dugongs, both placid browsers on sea grasses and floating vegetation.

Adaptations for aquatic life

Whales, seals and sirenians show many similar adaptations for life in water, with torpedo-shaped bodies streamlined by subdermal fat and flipper-like limbs. Fore-limbs contain the bony elements of the land-mammal's forearm, wrist and hand; seals retain similar hind limbs but whales and sirenians have lost them. In whales the rear half of the body is slender and flexible, broadening into two lateral flukes that beat up and down in the water with a slight spiralling twist. A big whale can swim at 25–30 km per hour, but usually

Seals (*above*) swim well, with little turbulence; dolphins (*below*) swim even better, sliding more smoothly through the water, with greater economy of effort

prefers a slower pace; dolphins can sprint at high speed or swim effortlessly at 10–20 km per hour. Seals use their hind ends and flippers as a propellor, steering and sometimes rowing with their fore-flippers. They swim elegantly but with less finesse than dolphins. Sirenians wag their hind ends too, ambling slowly through the water at a country-lane pace befitting sea cows.

Skeletons of all three groups show clearly their land ancestry, whales and sirenians departing furthest from the traditional pattern with their short necks, tapering bodies and much reduced pelvic girdles. Whales have spare skeletons, strong but lightweight, with spongy bones and strangely distorted skulls. Sirenians have massive skeletons and skulls, that may help to weigh them down in their shallow-water pastures.

Seals and sirenians are leathery-skinned; whales are rubbery, with a skin that dimples when they speed through the water, reducing friction. Most seals have coarse fur; fur seals alone have the beautiful velvety underfur that humans covet. All the aquatic mammals have a layer of subdermal blubber – fatty connective tissue that smooths their contours and helps keep them warm. Fur is a good insulator in air and shallow water but loses efficiency under pressure at depths. Whales abandoned it long ago in favour of thicker blubber which, permeated with blood vessels, provides variable insulation. Opening the vessels allows blood to flow freely and carry surplus heat to the skin for shedding. Constricting them reduces heat flow, and the blubber keeps the animal warm enough even lying at rest. Flippers and flukes too have variable blood supplies that control heat losses. Blubber is also a food reserve, allowing sea mammals to go without food when necessary.

Seals, sirenians and toothed whales (Odontoceti) have a short head and relatively small mouth, with a variety of teeth – cutting, crushing or holding, according to need. Teeth of many sea mammals grow annually, carrying within them a record of growth and age. Whalebone whales (Mysticeti) have no teeth or mere vestiges; instead the enormous mouth – in some species over a quarter of total body length – contains parallel sheets of whalebone, that filter minute animals from each mouthful of sea water. Whalebone too bears an annual record of growth, and so do minute waxy ear-plugs that several species carry; these all provide useful indications of age.

Seals often have large eyes appropriate for hunting in semi-darkness; sirenians and whales have smaller eyes protected by folds of skin. Only the sea lions and fur seals have external ear flaps, but all sea mammals hear well, mostly through bone conduction. Seals and whalebone whales carry sensory bristles on their faces that help them to detect prey close at hand. Walruses and Bearded Seals have especially impressive moustaches, used in feeling for clams and other prey in the soft mud of the sea bed.

All sea mammals breathe air. Muscular flaps close the nostrils automatically by reflex as they submerge. The nostrils of whales lie high on the head, at the point that first emerges when they surface. The throat and air passages are separate; whales cannot breathe through their mouth and have no vocal cords. Despite this they are surprisingly noisy animals with a repertoire of creaks, groans, whistles and chirruping songs that carry for miles through the water and sometimes sound clearly at the surface. Sirenians and seals too trill under

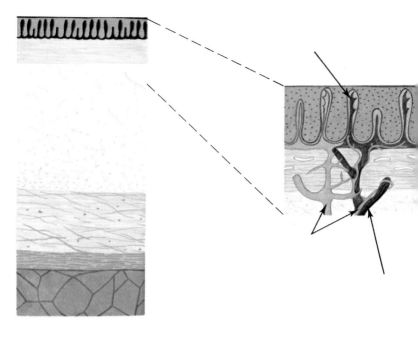

A whale's skin is multi-layered (*left*) with strata of fat (yellow) and tough connective tissue (blue) between the dermal layers (green) and muscles (brown). Blood supply to the skin can be varied (*right*): a resting whale constricts its dermal blood vessels (after Parry and Slijper)

water. Some of the calls are social, helping neighbours to keep in touch. Others are important in echo-location, detecting prey and underwater obstacles. Dolphin sonar is remarkably precise; in test conditions blindfolded animals can discriminate between their favourite small fish and other varieties the length of a tank away.

Lungs of sea mammals are elasticated and the air passages shaped for deep, rapid breathing. Whale lungs carry valves, and the air passages in the head are lined with oily foam. These two devices keep nitrogen from the bloodstream and so avoid 'bends', the painful eruption of gas bubbles into the blood when the animal rises from great depths. A whale's blow is a giant exhalation from the nostrils, carrying warm moist air and nitrogen-saturated foam from the lungs and air passages. Sea mammals take little air down with them when they dive, relying instead on oxygen stored in the red pigments of blood and muscles, with which they are well endowed. Relatively insensitive to carbon dioxide in their blood, they can stay below for well over an hour at rest, though less if they are hunting or swimming actively. During dives their heart-rate slows to a few beats per minute and blood is shunted from inessential organs to keep the brain supplied. Not generally deep divers, they mostly feed, swim and rest close to the surface. However, some seals have been recorded at depths of

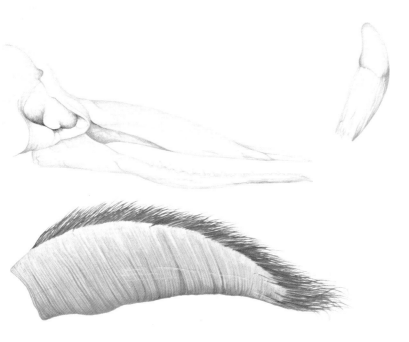

Skull of a sperm whale (*upper left*) showing the extensive jaws and relatively small cranium: there are peg-like teeth (right) only in the lower jaw

Baleen plate (*lower*) showing frayed edges and transverse growth bands. The age of a baleen whale can sometimes be estimated from these

five hundred metres and large toothed whales may hunt fish and squid at depths of a thousand metres or more.

Whales and sirenians mate, give birth and suckle their young in the water. Some species of seals mate in water, but all must come out on to land or sea ice to produce their pups, and only a few species are known to suckle in the sea. Seal and whale milk is rich and syrupy, with little sugar but plentiful fat. It promotes very rapid growth. The calves of some of the big whales, already over seven metres long at birth, double their length in six to nine months on mother's milk; some seals treble or quadruple their birth weight within two months. As for most mammals, the first year or two of life are the most hazardous, but sea mammals that survive infancy reach adolescence quickly (many large whales, for example, within two or three years), and live on into second, third or fourth decades.

Conservation

Marine mammals have long been preyed on by man for their meat, oil, hides, furs, whalebone and other useful products. Aboriginals often depended on them; a whale or a good catch of seals could keep an Arctic community alive through the winter. Industrial man became dependent in a different sense.

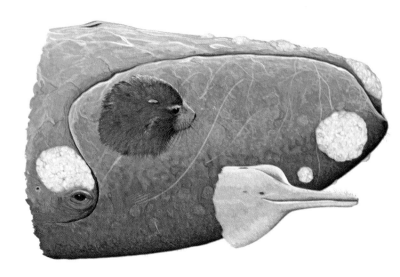

Head of a right whale; note the position of the eye (lower left) and nostril (upper left) and the huge lower jaw. The white patches are incrustations on which barnacles often grow. Inset are the dog-like head of a fur seal (*left*) and the more streamlined head of a river dolphin: note the sensory bristles on the tip

From the seventeenth century commercial whaling and sealing employed thousands on the hunting grounds and at home, and founded prosperous settlements from Norway to New Zealand. Marine mammals are hunted today; there are still small communities that welcome the fresh meat of a seal, walrus, dugong or dolphin, and there is still a commercial demand for seal furs and whale products. Now hunting is more efficient than ever before, and conservationists keep a sharp eye on it to guard against over-exploitation and possible extermination.

Commercial whaling is regulated by the International Whaling Commission (IWC), which works by securing agreement on levels of hunting to be permitted each year among its member-nations. Some species or stocks are given full protection, others are subject to quotas that come up for review periodically. Most species of large and medium-sized whales have been hunted at one time or another, some almost to extinction though none completely. Right, Grey, Humpback, Blue, Fin, Sei and Sperm Whales have all had their populations reduced, especially in recent decades by mobile fleets of factory ships and catchers operating on the high seas. Threatened species of Right, Grey and Blue Whales are currently protected by international agreement and many are now recovering. The other species are partly protected, along with some of the lesser whales on which hunting pressures have recently fallen.

IWC exercises useful control over the whaling of its own members, but works only by consensus (which is often difficult to reach), and cannot directly

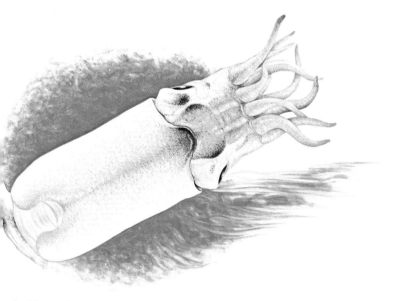

Squid: one of many species of shallow and deeper seas that form an important part of the diet of many whales and seals. Small ones are only a few centimetres long; the largest measure several metres, with grasping tentacles as long as the body

control the activities of non-member countries or protect whales against 'pirate' whalers. Conservationists who are concerned at the levels of whaling still permitted, and those who want to stop commercial whaling altogether, find other ways of achieving their ends – for example by pressing their own and other governments to provide whale sanctuaries, making it difficult for illicit whalers to insure their ships, intervening directly in whaling operations, and banning all trading in whale products.

Small whales too suffer their share of hunting, often by fishermen who complain (with truth) that they damage valuable nets and frighten away the fish. Whole schools of dolphins may be netted, harpooned or driven ashore for slaughtering. Hunting for meat is widespread too; Narwhals have suffered heavily in the Arctic, dolphin and porpoise populations in the Black Sea are much reduced by commercial hunters, and several species of river dolphins are now rare enough to cause concern. Then each year many thousands more dolphins die accidentally in fishing nets, and others are driven from their home waters by disturbance and pollution. Some stocks are large enough to stand these stresses, but several of the small whales are rare, or live in scattered groups that cannot be assessed. Any or all of them may be at risk from pressures put upon them by man.

Living closer to land, sirenians and seals are even more vulnerable to predation. Dugongs are steadily declining in numbers as man spreads further into their coastal haunts. Seals, especially fur seals, have been hunted for generations, and several species still attract the hunting gangs every year.

However, the commercially hunted species are hardly at risk; their numbers are high and frequently monitored, and the annual kill, under government licence and within limits set by national or international agreement, bears some relation (if not a very precise one) to the seals' natural capacity for replacement. Stocks of Northern Fur Seals have increased dramatically since 1911, when their hunting was rationalized under an international commission. South American Fur Seals on Lobos Island, Uruguay, have been managed successfully even for longer, and the annual killing of Harp and Hooded Seals in northern waters is unlikely to damage any of the hunted stocks beyond recovery.

Though the braining of several hundred thousand young seals for the sake of their skins is a matter of acute concern to humanitarians, the hunting of Harp and Hooded Seals is not the issue that most worries marine mammal conservationists today. Sea mammals breeding in huge, commercially exploitable stocks have shown remarkable capacity for recovery. As species they tend to breed young, and to adjust their reproductive rates to population pressures. With but a few exceptions they have been saved by the economic law of diminishing returns – as stocks diminish, hunting becomes more difficult and the hunters tend to seek other prey.

At much greater risk of extinction are small remnant stocks of warm-water seals – Monk Seals of the Mediterranean coast, for example, and Guadalupe and Galapagos Fur Seals of the eastern Pacific. Never plentiful, they are now very rare, and their tiny remnant stocks could die out accidentally or be killed off in casual ignorance by tourists or fishermen.

But a further hazard affects sea mammals of all kinds in every ocean, sea and estuary. The world's great water masses have become the world's great sewers and dumping grounds, and the material dumped contains poisons – mostly industrial wastes that are a direct product of human enterprise.

In open oceans the effect has so far been slight; their area is enormous and our best efforts have not yet produced enough rubbish to poison more than a fraction of them. But the human population continues to grow; industrial resources are mobilized and industrial wastes are flushed into the waterways in ever-increasing amounts. Many rivers, estuaries, fiords and shallow seas already show serious pollution; the Baltic, and parts of the Mediterranean and North Seas are prime examples.

Marine mammals suffer on three counts. Firstly, like seabirds they live close to the surface, where oil and other low-density pollutants gather. An oiled seal is no prettier than an oiled bird, and no less likely to die miserably before its time. Secondly, they are carnivores that accumulate toxins absorbed by their prey from surrounding waters, sickening and dying when the poisons reach lethal doses. Thirdly, they suffer when their prey are decimated or destroyed by poisons – when fish or clams are killed, when mussels and squid disappear from filthy, rubbish-filled waters.

Many industrial chemicals and products are implicated – the polychlorinated biphenyls, chlorinated hydrocarbons and organophosphates, for example, and such industrially important metals as lead, mercury and cadmium. Few marine birds or mammals in the world today are without traces of these products; many have measurable sublethal doses that are liable to become lethal when the animals are stressed by hunger or exhaustion. Even Antarctic seabirds and seals, far from centres of industry and civilization, are affected; infinitely more at risk are the small, local populations of narrow or land-locked seas – these cannot afford to lose numbers and cannot escape rising levels of pollution. If present trends continue, pollution will help to destroy stocks that are currently holding out against predation by man and other forms of interference; pollution is the last enemy that no marine mammal can withstand.

In general terms, sea mammals have so far managed to survive the impacts of a hungry, greedy and rapidly expanding humanity. We owe them much for their interest, lively presence and entertainment value; they owe us nothing, but depend on us more and more each year for their protection and well-being. We shall need our wits about us to see that they continue to survive and maintain their contribution to our enjoyment of the world.

Bears and otters

Order Carnivora
Suborder Arctoidea
Superfamily Canoidea

FAMILY URSIDAE

The bears are a family of large, omnivorous mammals, widespread and mainly terrestrial. Non-specialists, they walk on flat feet and are prepared to climb, dig, swim or (reluctantly) run after their food. Despite their bulk and a reputation for ferocity, bears are catholic feeders. Some are almost entirely herbivorous, others eat anything from roots and berries to birds' eggs, carrion and living prey. Several species haunt rivers, lakes and coasts in their constant search for food; only one – the Polar Bear – is truly maritime.

FAMILY URSIDAE
   Subfamily Ursinae
      Thalarctos maritimus

Polar Bear   *Thalarctos maritimus*   Phipps 1774

SIZE   Males: nose-to-tail length 2–2.5 (rarely 3) m, shoulder height 1–1.2 m; weight to 550 kg or more. Females 30–40 per cent smaller.
APPEARANCE   A large white or creamy-yellow bear, quite unmistakable for anything else. Short ears and tail: black eyes, nose and claws. Teeth $\frac{3\ 1\ 4\ 2-3}{3\ 1\ 4\ 2-3}$, sharp, flesh-eating.
RANGE   Coasts and ice-covered seas mainly north of the Arctic Circle, including North America (Bering Strait to northern Labrador), Greenland, northern Iceland, Svalband, much of the Soviet Arctic coast, and the Arctic Ocean. Migratory; over a dozen discrete populations are identified.

Typically coastal, Polar Bears live wherever their main food – Arctic seals – can be found. They wander alone or in small family groups, males and females staying together only briefly for mating in early spring. Pregnant females winter ashore or in dense offshore pack ice, digging dens in snow banks. Litters of two cubs (rarely one or three) are born in December or early January. Cubs are born blind, naked and rabbit-sized, weighing less than 1 kg. At three months, heavily furred and 10 kg in weight, they wander with mother over the pack-ice, hunting with her for two years or more before independence.

Polar Bears swim readily, taking seals and seabirds in the water. However, they hunt mostly on the ice itself, stalking sleeping seals, digging them from dens, or scooping them out of the water at breathing holes. In summer they forage ashore, especially in the Hudson Bay area, where they enter the forests. At human settlements they scavenge on rubbish tips, occasionally breaking into houses and stores in search of food.

Formerly an endangered species, Polar Bears are now protected by international agreement; there is a world population of 15,000–20,000. A few hundred are killed annually, mostly by traditional hunters under licence.

Polar Bears: (*above*) mother with two half-grown cubs crossing the sea ice; (*left*) waiting to grab a Ringed Seal at its breathing hole; (*below*) Polar Bears swim with a powerful 'dog-paddle' that keeps them moving slowly but strongly through the water

18

Sensitive facial bristles help the Sea Otter to hunt its prey in the water

FAMILY MUSTELIDAE

Otters are water-loving members of the family Mustelidae, the branch of the Carnivora that includes weasels, stoats, polecats, badgers and many other small-to-medium-sized predators. Generally grouped in a subfamily (Lutrinae) of their own, otters are lithe, semi-aquatic animals with long, slender bodies, short legs, tapering tails, webbed feet, and lively, inquiring dispositions. All live close to water, mostly in lakes, rivers and streams. Two marine species inhabit the western coastline of North and South America, one large and one small.

FAMILY MUSTELIDAE
  Subfamily Lutrinae
    Enhydra lutris
    Lutra felina

Sea Otter *Enhydra lutris* Linnaeus 1758

SIZE Head and body length to 1.2 m, tail to 36 cm. Males 25–40 kg; females usually slightly smaller.
APPEARANCE On land, large, sleek, chunky body, short legs, arched back and thick pointed tail. At sea, often floats on back with head raised. Fur dense, brown to black, with face, cheek, neck and whiskers paler. Blunt head, ears almost hidden, eyes small. Feet (especially hind feet) flipper-like, black. Teeth $\frac{3}{2}\frac{1}{1}\frac{3}{3}\frac{1}{2}$, including scissor-like carnassials for flesh-cutting.

Hunting on the sea bed in coastal shallows, Sea Otters blend well with their dark, dappled underwater environment

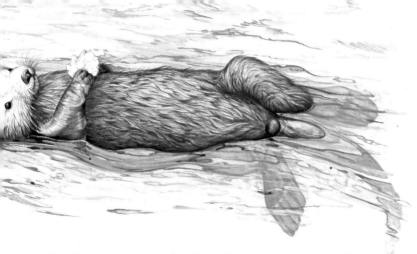

Air-breathing, like all other mammals, Sea Otters often bring food up to the surface;
here one breaks a hard-shelled clam against a stone on its chest

RANGE   Coastal north Pacific Ocean; in east, southern California to Aleutian Islands;
in west, Commander Islands, Kamchatka Peninsula and Kurile Islands. Three geographical races – eastern, northern and western – have been proposed.

Among the largest of the otters, this attractive creature was formerly one of
the commonest animals of northern Pacific coasts. Intensive hunting for its
splendid fur during the eighteenth and nineteenth centuries almost exterminated the species. Recovery began in 1910–11 under an international protection agreement, and numbers are now increasing again over parts of its former
range. It is most likely to be seen in coastal Alaska, Amchitka Island,
Vancouver Island, northern Washington and southern California. Sea Otters
spend much of their time in shallow coastal waters, among bays and sheltered
passages where kelp grows abundantly. They feed on the sea bed, diving for
about a minute at a time in search of clams, crabs, starfish and sea urchins,
hunting as much by touch as by sight or smell. Californian Sea Otters have
recently learned to investigate discarded beer cans which, littering the sea
floor, are often the home of small octopus or abalones. For long they have been
known to tuck clams and other hard shellfish under their arm, bring them to
the surface and break them against stones, using their chest as an anvil.
Between feeds they sleep on their backs in the water, snoring gently with arms
folded elegantly across the chest. They mate at sea in spring and early summer;
pups (usually single, rarely twins) are born ashore eight to nine months later,
probably after a period of delayed implantation. The pups are carried to sea
immediately and swim alongside their mother for a year or more. Moaning or
bleating calls link parent and young. Current world population is estimated at
125,000.

Marine Otters live in coastal waters of southern Chile. They are hunted severely for their beautiful furs

Marine Otter   *Lutra felina*   (Molina 1782) (not illustrated)

SIZE   Head and body length 57–79 cm, tail 30–36 cm. Weight of one male 4.1 kg. Sexes probably similar.
APPEARANCE   A small, dark grey-brown otter with grizzled back and flanks; cheeks, throat and undersurface paler. Fur harsh; feet partly webbed.
RANGE   Formerly in coastal waters of western South America from about 9°S in central Peru to the tip of southern Chile. Now very rare in Peru, and restricted in Chile almost entirely to the south of 42°S.

This tiny coastal and riverine otter, attractively named *chungungo* on its home ground, formerly occupied an enormous length of coastline from the tropics to cold temperate Tierra del Fuego. Constant hunting has now restricted it virtually to the heavily wooded islands and mainland coasts of southern Chile, though a small population of two or three hundred may also persist in central Peru. Its ecology is little known, though it seems to occupy a shore and shallow-water niche similar to that of the Sea Otter in the north. Food includes molluscs, shrimps both marine and freshwater, and shallow-water fish. Chungungos live solitarily, spaced out along the coasts; parents meet only briefly to mate about midsummer, and litters of two are born in late autumn. Though officially protected, Marine Otters seem still to be caught, killed and skinned wherever they appear, and their skins find good prices on illegal markets.

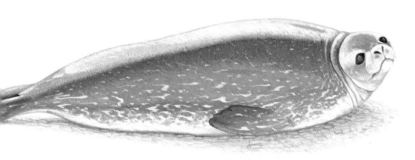

Weddell Seal (Phocidae)

Seals, sea lions and walruses

ORDER PINNIPEDIA

These groups are usually considered sufficiently like each other, and unlike other mammals, to merit an order of their own; some taxonomists, however, rate them only as one or more sea-going suborders within the order Carnivora. There are three families – the 'earless' seals (Phocidae), the 'eared' seals (Otariidae) and the Walruses (Odobaenidae). Eared seals and Walruses are closely akin and thought to have evolved from bear-like ancestors; their families are joined in the superfamily Otarioidea. Earless seals stand slightly

Californian Sea Lion (Otariidae)

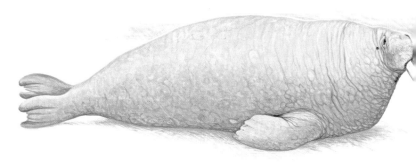

Walrus (Odobaenidae)

apart, and are thought to have evolved from otter-like ancestors; for symmetry the single family Phocidae is given a superfamily of its own (Phocidea). Earless or eared, the seals have evolved much further towards aquatic life than any bear or otter existing today, though they remain more land-bound and less adroit in the water than their aquatic rivals, the whales.

SUPERFAMILY PHOCIDEA

FAMILY PHOCIDAE

Earless or 'true' seals have no external ear flaps (pinnae), though they hear perfectly well in water or air. Their hind flippers cannot be turned forward, and their fore-flippers are short – more like paddles than legs – and furry all over. There are well-developed nails on the flippers, used for scratching, and the testes are hidden away within the body. The coat, short and bristly, is often sleek but never velvety. On land or sea ice they crawl, some pulling themselves along with flexed fore-limbs, others humping their fat, unwieldy bodies like over-fed caterpillars. They can travel surprising distances over gravel and rocks – Antarctic phocids are sometimes found several miles inland, though usually in circumstances suggesting they are lost or distressed. But phocids are at their best in water, where their weight becomes negligible and their streamlined shape makes them by far the most efficient of all seals. Living phocids fall into two clear subfamilies, the Phocinae of the Arctic and neighbouring seas, and the Monachinae of temperate, tropical and southern waters.

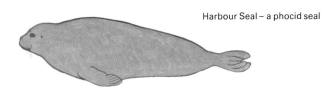

Harbour Seal – a phocid seal

FAMILY PHOCIDAE

Subfamily Phocinae

Phoca vitulina (5 races)	Harbour Seal
Pusa hispida (6 races)	Ringed Seal
Pusa sibirica	Baikal Seal
Pusa caspica	Caspian Seal
Halichoerus grypus	Grey Seal
Histriophoca fasciata	Ribbon Seal
Pagophilus groenlandicus	Harp Seal
Erignathus barbatus (2 races)	Bearded Seal
Cystophora cristata	Hooded Seal

Subfamily Monachinae

Monachus monachus	Mediterranean Monk Seal
Monachus tropicalis	Caribbean Monk Seal
Monachus schauinslandi	Hawaiian Monk Seal
Ommatophoca rossi	Ross Seal
Lobodon carcinophagus	Crabeater Seal
Hydrurga leptonyx	Leopard Seal
Leptonychotes weddelli	Weddell Seal
Mirounga leonina	Southern Elephant Seal
Mirounga angustirostris	Northern Elephant Seal

SUBFAMILY PHOCINAE

Seals of this subfamily characteristically have three incisors on either side of the upper jaw. The digits of the hind flippers are almost equal in length and carry prominent claws; those of the front flippers may be used in pulling the animal forward over snow or ice. The pups have a white natal coat. All nine species live in the north. Two (Ringed and Bearded Seals) are circumpolar, breeding far north on the pack-ice. Three species (Harp, Hooded and Ribbon Seals) breed mainly on the pack-ice edge, dispersing northward as the edge retreats in summer. Grey and Harbour Seals keep mainly to cool temperate waters; Baikal and Caspian Seals are restricted to their own inland waters.

Harbour Seals

Harbour or Common Seal *Phoca vitulina* Linnaeus 1758

SIZE Males: nose-to-tail length 1.6–1.9 m, weight to 120 kg. Females average 10 per cent smaller.

APPEARANCE A small, fat, round-headed seal. Colour variable; leaden-grey with dark spots, darker grey with pale spots, sandy or dark brown; sometimes slightly paler underneath. Pups have, first, a soft white fur, normally shed before or at birth, followed by blue-grey fur, paler on the underparts, which lasts almost a year until the first moult. Teeth $\frac{3\,1\,2\,3}{3\,1\,2\,3}$; cheek teeth strongly cusped, set slightly obliquely in jaw.

RANGE Five geographical races are identified: (i) *P.v. vitulina*, Europe from northern Spain to North Cape and Iceland; (ii) *P.v. concolor*, North America from Maine to Ellesmere Islands, western and southern Greenland; (iii) *P.v. mellonae*, a small stock in freshwater lakes east of Hudson Bay; (iv) *P.v. richardi*, eastern Pacific and Arctic Oceans from southern California to the north coast of Alaska, including the Aleutian Islands; (v) *P.v. largha*, western Pacific Ocean from Korea and southern Japan to Bering Strait.

Harbour Seals are small, shy, coastal and estuarine seals, found mainly in sandy bays, sea lochs and shallows – sometimes on shelving rocky coasts, seldom on steep ones. Sociable but not colonial, they rarely come ashore. Though occasionally found resting on beaches, their favourite haunts for hauling out are sandbanks and rocky ledges exposed at low tide. Fish eaters, they often fall foul of inshore fishermen, with whom they compete.

Breeding groups gather in sheltered waters from spring to late summer, dates varying with race and locality. Courtship is boisterous, displaying males leaping like salmon from the water. Embryos implant after a delay of ten weeks. Pups of *P.v. largha* are born mostly on ice-floes between February and April, retaining their white downy coats. Those of other races are born in May and June, on sandbanks and rock shelves at low tide. The pups are large and well-formed, and able to swim alongside their mothers only hours later. They reach independence in five to six weeks, having trebled their birth weight in that period. Tens of thousands – mostly yearlings – are taken annually for their skins. World population of Common Seals probably approaches half a million.

Harbour Seal in juvenile coat, worn throughout its first year

Brown and grey colour phases of Harbour Seals: this is a variable species, ranging from silver to dark brown or black

Ribbon Seal   *Histriophoca fasciata*   (Zimmermann 1783)

SIZE   Males: nose-to-tail length 1.8–2 m, weight to 90 kg. Females slightly smaller.
APPEARANCE   A small, dark brown seal, snub-nosed, with distinctive ribbon-like bands of white or creamy-yellow about the neck, flanks and pelvis. Females are paler than males, with ribbons less sharply defined. Pups white at birth. Teeth $\frac{3\ 1\ 4\ 1}{2\ 1\ 4\ 1}$, small, widely spaced, with accessory cusps.
RANGE   North Pacific Ocean. Found on the winter sea ice off Sakhalin Island (especially the northern Tatar Strait), Shantarskiye Island, the northern Sea of Okhotsk, Kamchatka, the western Bering Sea, and the Arctic coast of the USSR to Ayon Island. It is also known from St Lawrence Island, the Pribilof Islands, Cape Prince of Wales and Norton Bay, and rarely from the Aleutians.

Not rare (population estimated at twenty to fifty thousand), and familiar to hunters throughout its range, this little brown and white seal of the Pacific ice-floes is among those least known to scientists. Few naturalists have spent more than a few hours obser ng behaviour and estimating numbers. Little is known of its summer moveme. when the pack-ice has broken and dispersed.
    Ribbon Seals are reported to gather on sea ice close to the land in early spring, giving birth to their pups in March and early April. The pups shed their downy coats in late April and May, achieving independence as the sea ice disperses. Mating occurs in small colonies on the last remnants of pack-ice in summer. The diet includes fish, squid and crustaceans.

Ringed Seal   *Pusa hispida*   (Schreber 1775)

SIZE   Male: nose-to-tail length 1.2–1.8 m; weight to 130 kg. Sexes similar, males on average slightly larger.
APPEARANCE   Small, fat, round-headed: colour dull grey-brown with large dark spots (often white-ringed), merging to blotches and stripes on the back; underside paler, speckled. Fur coarse, stiff; prominent yellow-brown whiskers. Pups born white, acquiring grey coat at one month. Teeth $\frac{3\ 1\ 4\ 1}{2\ 1\ 4\ 1}$; cheek teeth conical with two small cusps.
RANGE   Circumpolar Arctic, generally among pack-ice. Six geographical races: (i) *P.h. hispida*, polar basin, Greenland, northern Iceland, Labrador, Canadian archipelago, northern Scandinavia; (ii) *P.h. krascheninikovi*, northern Bering Sea and eastern Kamchatka; (iii) *P.h. ochotensis*, Okhotsk Sea, western Kamchatka, Sakhalin and northern Japan; (iv) *P.h. botnica*, Baltic Sea, Gulf of Bothnia and Finland; (v) *P.h. saimensis*, Lake Saimaa, Finland; (vi) *P.h. ladogensis*, Lake Ladoga, Finland. The last two may be variants of *P.h. botnica.* Non-migratory; stragglers have been recorded off northern Britain.

This is a seal of inshore ice, probably the commonest and certainly the most widespread Arctic species. It feeds on the larger crustaceans of the plankton and small fish caught in shallow water at depths down to a hundred metres. Sociable but not colonial, Ringed Seals gather to mate in April, where pups are still being suckled on the nursery ice. The embryos implant in August, and the pups are born seven to eight months later in March and April, usually in snow caverns or sheltered hollows of the ice-field. Though safe from casual predators, they may be dug out by Arctic Foxes or Polar Bears. Adults maintain winter breathing holes in the ice, where they are vulnerable both to Polar Bears and to Eskimo harpoons. World population is estimated at two to six million. Many thousands – mostly pups – are killed each year for the fur trade.

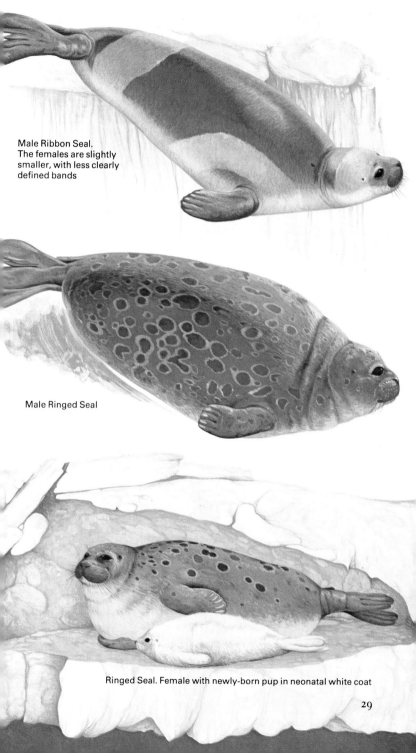

Male Ribbon Seal.
The females are slightly
smaller, with less clearly
defined bands

Male Ringed Seal

Ringed Seal. Female with newly-born pup in neonatal white coat

Baikal Seal *Pusa sibirica* (Gmelin 1788)

SIZE Nose-to-tail length 1.5 m, weight to 65 kg. Sexes similar.
APPEARANCE Small seals, silver-grey to olive-brown dorsally, flanks and belly paler.
Pups are born with yellowish-white fur, moulting to silver-grey after two to three weeks.
Teeth $\frac{3\ 1\ 4\ 1}{2\ 1\ 4\ 1}$; cheek teeth with four or five cusps.
RANGE Confined to Lake Baikal, Siberia, especially the northern end; occasionally
also in neighbouring rivers.

Among the smallest seals, the Baikal Seal is similar to the Ringed Seal of the
Arctic, more so to the equally isolated Caspian Seal. All three probably
originated from common stock in the mid-Tertiary when inland seas covered
more of Asia than at present. Subject to one of the world's harshest winter
climates, Baikal Seals spend October to May under or among the ridged lake
ice. From December to February few are seen. Gravid females live hidden in
snow-covered dens that open directly to the water; males and non-breeding
females avoid the coldest weather by staying in the lake, breathing through
cracks and blow-holes. Single or twin pups, covered in dense white fur, are
born in the dens during March. In April and May the seals emerge on to the ice
to sun themselves, dropping back into the lake at the least sign of danger. In
June, as the ice disperses and the pups reach independence, adults herd
together in remote parts of the lake for mating.

Baikal Seals feed mainly on fish. Of a world population estimated at
50,000–100,000, roughly one tenth are killed each year for food and pelts.

Caspian Seal *Pusa caspica* (Gmelin 1788)

SIZE Males: nose to tail 1.6 m, weight 85 kg. Females slightly smaller.
APPEARANCE Small seals, yellow-brown to olive-grey, with elongate dorsal spots and
patches. Pups are born with white fur, which is replaced in the fourth week by a fleecy
grey juvenile coat. Teeth $\frac{3\ 1\ 4\ 1}{2\ 1\ 4\ 1}$ cheek teeth triangular, spaced, with small cusps.
RANGE Restricted entirely to the Caspian Sea, occasionally entering neighbouring
rivers. Migratory, spending winters in the pack-ice of the northern Caspian, summers in
the desert-fringed south.

Similar in size to Ringed and Baikal Seals, and intermediate in colour, these
small phocids are thought to be another relict population, isolated during
geological upheavals of the last few million years. Apparently very successful
(they may total almost a million), Caspian Seals face the greatest annual
climatic swing of any species. In autumn they migrate in large herds to the cold
shallows of the north-eastern Caspian, hauling out on to the ice as soon as it
forms. There, in the semi-polar conditions of January and February, the
females gather in groups of several hundred and produce their pups. Holes
and leads in the ice give them constant access to the water. Pups enter the sea at
four to five weeks and quickly gain independence; like the adults, they feed
mostly on fish. In late February and March males join the nursery groups,
pairing off with the females and mating. As the ice disperses both sexes
undergo a complete moult. Then the herds move southward to the deeper end
of the Caspian, where, despite the tropical climate, upwelling currents provide
cool surface waters and plentiful food throughout the summer.

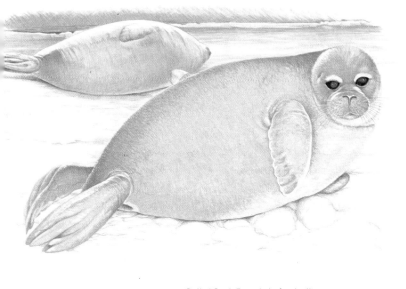

Baikal Seal. Female in fresh silver-grey coat.
These occur only in Siberia's Lake Baikal

Caspian Seal.
A 'ringed' species
now restricted to the
Caspian Sea

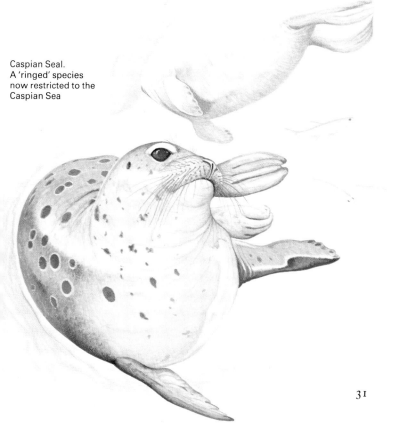

Grey Seal   *Halichoerus grypus*   (Fabricius 1791)

SIZE   Males: nose-to-tail length to 3.0 m, weight 250–280 kg. Females 10–15 per cent smaller.

APPEARANCE   Large mottled seals; in males the mottling is dark grey on a fawn background, in females pale grey on a darker background, with relatively pale face and belly. The convex 'Roman' nose is distinctive. Pups have a white woolly coat for three weeks, then blue-grey fur. Teeth $\frac{3\ 1\ 4\ 1}{3\ 1\ 4\ 1}$.

RANGE   North Atlantic, in three discrete but little-differentiated populations – (i) Britain, Norway, White Sea, Iceland and Faeroe Islands; (ii) Baltic Sea; (iii) Gulf of St Lawrence, Newfoundland, and the neighbouring waters.

These are seals of rocky shores and troubled waters, found typically among islands and reefs of exposed coasts. They are the characteristic seals of Britain's northern and western isles, though common too on the sandbanks and beaches of the North Sea. Britain's stocks of Grey Seals, now estimated at over thirty-five thousand and probably growing, include half to two thirds of the world's population.

Mainly fish eaters, Grey Seals feed at all depths down to a hundred metres or more, diving for spells of up to twenty minutes. Their diet includes flatfish, molluscs and other creatures of the sea bed, and a proportion of commercial fish that makes many fishermen their enemies. Sociable and colonial, they haul out in the autumn in large, untidy breeding groups, usually on remote islands. In the eastern Atlantic most pups are born between September and December, in the Gulf of St Lawrence from late January to March, though breeding may occur in any month of the year. Bulls fight in rivalry over territories as the first pups of the season appear, and the cows are ready for mating even before their offspring of the year are weaned. When breeding is over both adults and young return to the sea independently, older seals hauling out again in late spring to complete their moult.

Grey Seal. Adults are distinguishable by the convex 'Roman' nose, pups (*below*) by their woolly grey neonatal down

Harp Seal *Pagophilus groenlandicus* (Erxleben 1777)

SIZE   Males: length nose to tail 1.8 m; weight to 180 kg. Females slightly smaller.
APPEARANCE   A small- to medium-sized piebald seal. In males the fur is white or straw-coloured, the face black or dark brown, and a ring, 'harp', or horseshoe of coalescing dark spots decorates the back. Females and young are grey, usually with a less distinctive pattern of dark spots and a paler muzzle; older females, like the one in the illustration, have darker head and flank patches similar to those of the male. Pups are born in white woolly fur, which is replaced at three to four months with fine grey fur that grows progressively more spotted throughout their first year; thereafter the markings tend to increase and darken with age. Teeth $\frac{3\ 1\ 4\ 1}{2\ 1\ 4\ 1}$, small, well spaced apart.
RANGE   Arctic and North Atlantic, breeding on deep-water ice-fields centred in the southern Barents Sea, the Greenland Sea, the Gulf of St Lawrence, and off Labrador. Migratory over the Atlantic north of 60°N and neighbouring sections of the Arctic Ocean, and an occasional visitor to Britain and Western Europe.

These are seals of open water and pack-ice, seldom found ashore or close to land. Pelagic feeders, they browse throughout summer in the rich surface waters of the high Arctic and the sub-Arctic, taking plankton and schooling fish. As the ice forms in late autumn they head south towards their traditional breeding grounds, hauling out in the middle of large fields of hummocky pack-ice, where they are protected from wave action and from the attentions of Killer Whales. Pups are born off eastern Greenland in late March, elsewhere in late February or March. Males join the colonies as the pups are born; mating occurs two to three weeks later as the pups shed their white coats and enter the sea for the first time.

With a huge population, possibly totalling five million, this is the most heavily hunted of all the world's seals. Some hundreds of thousands of pups and young animals are taken by commercial hunters each year, mostly for their fur. Local stocks are reduced from time to time, but the species as a whole does not appear to be endangered; nor is it likely to be while the main centres of breeding are protected by bastions of fast ice which small vessels cannot enter. Public protest based on the cruelty of the annual slaughter has so far had little effect. Pups and juveniles will no doubt continue to be killed so long as there remains a flourishing market for their skins.

Harp Seal. The male in the background is typically marked. The female (with pup) is greyer, with less clearly defined dorsal markings. This one has an all-dark face mask; many females have a paler mask with grey muzzle. The dark patches may be black or deep tan; in males the background varies from dark to pale straw-colour (*lower left*), fading to very pale straw in summer

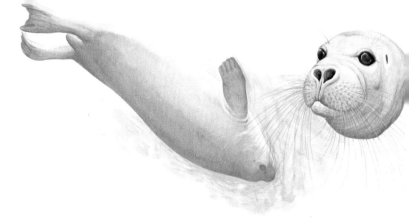

Bearded Seal. The long vibrissae – straight (*above*) or crimped when dry (*below right*) – are used to detect prey on the sea bed. Pup of two weeks in natal coat. See below

Bearded Seal   *Erignathus barbatus*   (Erxleben 1777)

SIZE   Males: nose-to-tail length 2.5–3.0 m; weight to 400 kg. Females slightly smaller.
APPEARANCE   Large seals with plain fur, only weakly mottled or spotted; cinnamon-brown on back, greyish or yellow flanks, underside and flippers. Fore-flippers square-cut, with strong black claws. Strikingly bushy moustache of yellow whiskers, long and curved; heavy lower jaw. Four mammae. Teeth $\frac{3\ 1\ 4\ 1}{3\ 1\ 4\ 1}$; molars often worn down to stumps.
RANGE   Circumpolar Arctic. Two races are distinguished: (i) *E.b. barbatus*, Arctic coast from Laptev Sea westward to northern Scandinavia; Greenland, north-eastern Canada to Hudson Bay and Gulf of St Lawrence; (ii) *E.b. nautica*, Arctic coast of north-east Asia, Kamchatka, Sea of Okhotsk, Sakhalin Island, Kurile Islands, northern Bering Sea, Arctic coasts of Alaska and Canada.

Among the largest of the northern seals, the Bearded Seal makes its home on moving inshore ice, in shallow coastal waters where the sea bed is rich in food. Like its distant cousin the Walrus, this seal is a bottom feeder, sometimes hunting at depths of a hundred metres or more. The 'beard' – more accurately a curly moustache – is highly sensory, presumably used for detecting food on a muddy sea bed. The worn teeth, typical of most adults, testify to a diet that includes many hard-shelled crustaceans and molluscs.

Rather solitary animals, Bearded Seals lie widely scattered across the sea ice in April and May when the pups are born. Over a metre long at birth, the grey-coated pups seem to spend several more weeks with their mothers than those of other Arctic species, so mature females usually mate only in alternate years. World population is estimated at a hundred to a hundred and fifty thousand; too widely dispersed to attract the commercial hunters, they are of interest mainly to Eskimos and other local hunters, who value their tough hides for traces, bindings and boot leather.

Hooded Seal. Typically dark silver-grey, these may also be heavily suffused with brown. Face and flippers are always darker than the rest of the body, even in the pups (*middle*). Males have an inflatable proboscis, used in threat display during fighting on the breeding floes

Hooded Seal   *Cystophora cristata*   (Erxleben 1777)

SIZE   Males: nose-to-tail length 3–3.5 m, weighing to 400 kg or more; females are slightly smaller.

APPEARANCE   Large silver-grey seals, splashed irregularly with dark grey or black spots. Face dark; in adult males the upper surface of the nose and forehead is inflatable, producing a bulbous profile – possibly a threat-signal for rivals. Claws unusually prominent, especially on the fore-flippers. Teeth $\frac{2\,1\,5}{1\,1\,5}$; cheek teeth are widely spaced pegs.

RANGE   A seal of North Atlantic and Arctic Ocean sea ice, found from Newfoundland and Baffin Land in the west to Spitzbergen, Jan Mayen and Iceland in the east, usually on stable pack-ice in offshore waters. Vagrants have been recorded from as far south as Florida, Britain and the Bay of Biscay. There are two main breeding centres – a small one between Labrador and Greenland, and a larger one north of Jan Mayen Island; smaller groups breed in the Gulf of St Lawrence and Davis Strait.

Seldom found inshore, Hooded Seals live well out to sea, feeding on plankton and fish mostly in surface waters, and hauling out on to the floes to rest. They gather in huge groups on the stable winter ice of the breeding areas in March and April, pairing off as the silvery-grey pups are born. Mating occurs two to three weeks after birth, and the family groups disperse some three weeks later. Throughout summer many Hooded Seals moult on the heavy pack-ice between Greenland and Iceland; in winter they are spread thinly wherever there is open water for them to feed. The large breeding concentrations are subject to controlled hunting under international agreement; tens of thousands of pups are taken each year for their fleecy coats, and as many adults for their oil and leather. The total population, estimated mainly from aerial counts, probably exceeds 500,000.

Sea lion, discussed
on page 53

SUBFAMILY MONACHINAE

Monachine seals typically have two incisors on either side of the upper jaw and two below; elephant seals are exceptional with only one below. On the hind flippers the two outer digits are notably longer than the middle three and the claws tend to be small. The pups have grey, brown or black natal coats. There are nine species. The three monk seals live in warm northern-hemisphere waters – of the Mediterranean Sea and neighbouring eastern Atlantic Ocean, the Caribbean islands, and the Hawaiian chain. Northern Elephant Seals too are a warm-water species, living off Mexico and California. The rest are southern seals of cold or icy water. Weddell Seals live coastally on the fast ice of the Antarctic continent and neighbouring islands, Ross and Crabeater Seals pelagically in the heart of the pack-ice; Leopard Seals commute between pack-ice edge and cold temperate zone, and Southern Elephant Seals are a cold-temperate and sub-Antarctic species.

Mediterranean Monk Seal *Monachus monachus* (Hermann 1779)

SIZE   Males: nose-to-tail length 2.8–3.3 m; weight of large animals over 300 kg. Females similar or slightly smaller.

APPEARANCE   A large, substantial seal with short bristly fur; usually chocolate or dark brown dorsally with irregular paler patches and spots, shading ventrally to fawn or yellow-grey. Pups similar, with longer, softer fur; old adults may be silvery. Teeth $\frac{2\,1\,5}{2\,1\,5}$; molars oblique with high central cusp.

RANGE   Widely but thinly distributed in the Mediterranean and Black Seas and along the coast of north-west Africa to Cap Blanc, Madeira and the Canary Islands.

A secretive species, forming small breeding groups in caverns on rocky coasts. The single young, born in September and October, are weaned after five weeks. A longer-than-annual cycle probably requires females to breed only in alternate years. This was once a common seal. Classical writers mentioned it, coins portrayed it, and a scattering of place-names from Madeira to Turkey tell of its former abundance. Today it is rare; though still present over much of its former range, the Mediterranean Monk Seal is an endangered species, hunted as a traditional enemy by inshore fishermen and safe only in a very few protected areas. Recent surveys have shown it to be almost completely absent from the north shores of the western Mediterranean, very thinly scattered in Morocco, Algeria and Tunisia, rare in the Balearics, and almost eliminated from Corsica and Sardinia. There are small breeding colonies in Madeira, Rio de Oro, Yugoslavia and the eastern Aegean Sea. World population is estimated at 400–800 only.

Hawaiian Monk Seal *Monachus schauinslandi* (Matschie 1905)

SIZE   Nose-to-tail length 2.4–2.8 m; weight about 170 kg. Sexes similar.

APPEARANCE   Sleek grey or grey-brown seals with paler, silvery undersurface; the fur may be tinged green with algal growth. Teeth $\frac{2\,1\,5}{2\,1\,5}$; similar to those of *M. tropicalis.*

RANGE   Breed on six coral atolls (Kure, Midway, Pearl and Hermes Reef, Lisianski Island, Laysan Island and French Frigates Shoal) in the Leeward Islands of the Hawaiian chain. Rarely seen elsewhere.

This small population, estimated at about a thousand, is all that remains of a once-plentiful species subjected to remorseless hunting. Hawaiian Monk Seals, far removed from their nearest kin in the Caribbean, survive on a few isolated atolls and beaches, as far as possible from their arch-enemy, man. They feed locally about their reefs and islands on squid, octopus, conger eels and flat-fish which they catch mostly at night. Mating behaviour is seen in the small colonies between March and early July. Single, black-furred pups are born between December and August (mostly in April and May) weighing 15–17 kg. They may swim shortly after birth, and are often in the water at a week to ten days. During five weeks of lactation the mothers starve while the pups almost quadruple their birth weight. As yearlings they slim down to about 45 kg. Sharks are believed to be a major predator.

Mediterranean
Monk Seal

Dark-coloured pups are
characteristic of the Monachinae subfamily

Hawaiian Monk Seal.
Only about one thousand
of these seals remain on their
northern Pacific islands

Caribbean Monk Seal   *Monachus tropicalis*   (Gray 1850) (not illustrated)

SIZE   Males: nose-to-tail length 2.4–2.8 m; weight unknown. Females slightly smaller.
APPEARANCE   A quiet, lethargic species, dark greyish-brown on the back, yellow or yellowish-white underneath, especially in males. Fur only about 1 cm long, sometimes green from algal growth. Pups black, with long woolly fur which they lose on weaning. Teeth $\frac{2\,1\,5}{2\,1\,5}$; molars straight, with waist and low central cusp, and a rough crown.
RANGE   Formerly present on islands of the northern and central Caribbean Sea, including the Bahamas, Cuba, Haiti, Jamaica, Pedro Cay, Alta Vela, Guadeloup, and Alacrane and the Triangles Islands off Yucatan. Now nearly or completely extinct.

Once an abundant species, Caribbean Monk Seals have been hunted for oil and pelts for well over three hundred years. Towards the end of the last century, when they were still fairly plentiful, they were reported to breed in small groups, pupping in December. There is still a slight hope that a few may exist on some of the thousands of reefs and atolls within their former range; anyone knowing of their existence would be wise to keep quiet about it, unless the long-term safety of the colony could be absolutely assured. However, the chances of survival of any of this species are remote indeed.

Ross Seal   *Ommatophoca rossi*   (Gray 1844)

SIZE   Nose-to-tail length 1.8–2.3 m; weight up to 200 kg. Sexes similar in size.
APPEARANCE   Dark grey or grey-brown on the head, back and flanks, silver-grey underneath. The head is small, with seemingly tiny mouth; the eyes are large, bulging under the skin. When disturbed, Ross Seals trill musically and pull their head back into the fat of the neck, in a way that led early naturalists to think they had inflatable throat pouches. Teeth $\frac{2\,1\,3\,2}{2\,1\,3\,1}$; cheek teeth small, sharply cusped and well spaced.
RANGE   Circumpolar within the Antarctic pack-ice; not yet reported elsewhere.

This strangely elusive seal was first recorded in the 1840s and for long regarded as a rarity; fewer than fifty had been seen a century later, and only about two hundred up to 1970. Then powerful ice-breakers, forging through the pack-ice with helicopters in attendance, made possible a truer picture. Ross Seals share Antarctic pack-ice with their much more numerous cousins the Crabeater Seals. They live singly or in very small, widely scattered groups, rarely north of 60°S. Their food is probably large squid, caught at depth below the ice-floes. They pup in November and December, and are likely to mate one to two months later. Despite their apparent rarity, censuses suggest a substantial population of between 50,000 and 150,000.

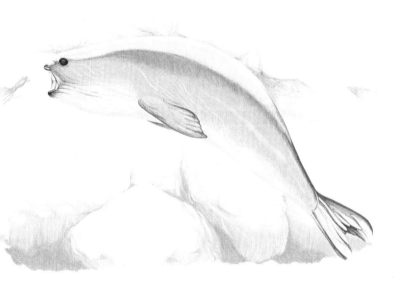

Ross Seal. An elegant species of the Antarctic pack-ice (see also p. 49)

Crabeater Seal   *Lobodon carcinophagus*   (Hombron and Jacquinot 1842)

SIZE   Males: nose-to-tail length 2.8–3 m, weighing 250–300 kg. Females similar or slightly larger.

APPEARANCE   Silver-grey to fawn, uniform or paler below; flanks often scarred by deep parallel cuts of Killer Whale teeth. Teeth $\frac{2\,1\,3\,2}{2\,1\,3\,2}$; the outer incisors of the upper jaw are almost as big as the canines, and the five cheek teeth have additional cusps, giving them a distinctive saw-like profile.

RANGE   Circumpolar within the Antarctic pack-ice, ranging south to the inshore ice of the Antarctic continent and Peninsula; vagrants are occasionally reported from the cold temperate islands, Australia and South America.

These slender, elegant animals, almost entirely confined to the shifting pack-ice of the far south, are probably the most numerous of all seals. They are certainly among the least known, for ships seldom penetrate the denser regions of the pack-ice and biologists have had few opportunities to study them. They feed mostly on krill, which is abundant in surface waters among the pack-ice in summer; their slotted cheek teeth are thought to be effective in sifting small organisms from the sea. While feeding they are especially vulnerable to attacks by Killer Whales; many bear the scars of close encounters. Little is known of their breeding, but they are believed to form family pairs (rather than harems), the pups are born in spring (September to November), and mating probably occurs after the pups are weaned three to six weeks later. Annual migrations almost certainly occur, though their pattern is unknown. The total population has been estimated at 50–75 million.

Not surprisingly Crabeater Seals have from time to time been considered for commercial exploitation. Their pelts are no less desirable than those of other hair-seals; because of their diet, their meat is free from parasitic cysts and fishy taint, and has an excellent flavour. However, their wide dispersion and the dangers of the southern pack-ice make hunting unprofitable. Small ships would be inefficient, large ones too costly to use; until someone finds a cheaper and safer method of taking them, Crabeater Seals have little to fear from man.

Crabeater Seal. Restricted mainly to the Antarctic pack-ice and probably the world's most numerous seal, with a population of over fifty million

Leopard Seal   *Hydrurga leptonyx*   (Blainville 1820)

SIZE   Males: nose-to-tail length 2.8–3.2 m; weight up to about 270 kg. Females slightly bigger on average, the largest up to 3.8 m.

APPEARANCE   Lithe silver-grey seals, dark above and light below, liberally sprinkled with slate-grey spots. The long neck, snake-like head, inquisitive air and wide, toothy grin are all distinctive. Teeth $\frac{2\ 1\ 3\ 2}{2\ 1\ 3\ 2}$; the cheek teeth have saw-like additional cusps.

RANGE   Widespread at the northern edge of the Antarctic pack-ice in summer, ranging north to the sub-Antarctic and cool temperate islands in winter; a fairly frequent visitor to Australia, New Zealand and southern South America.

Leopard Seals are animals of character – lively on land as well as at sea, with a reputation for cunning and ferocity. Solitary animals, they are often seen sleeping peacefully on floes or beaches, sometimes surrounded by other kinds of seals or groups of nonchalant penguins. In the water they are active hunters, chasing fish, penguins and possibly the young of other seals. Large flippers and a slender body give them an unusual turn of speed. Often one or two establish themselves for a season close to a penguin colony, catching the birds as they come in from fishing, and killing and skinning the carcases by beating them expertly against the sea. Curious but timid, they investigate strange objects closely, playing with timbers and popping up alarmingly alongside small boats. Shouting or banging is usually enough to keep them away. Little is known of their family life; they breed on the pack-ice about midsummer, and the young of the year take part in the annual northward migration. A total population of 250,000–500,000 has been estimated.

Because of their reputed ferocity, Leopard Seals are feared by polar visitors and often shot on sight. This is unfortunate; I know no record of their attacking humans on land or sea ice, and no authenticated record of attacks on boats. But they can be disconcerting; on snow they can slither much faster than a man can run, and will move towards anyone who comes between them and their escape route to the sea. In the water they approach small boats very closely; to have a large Leopard Seal resting its chin on the stern of a dinghy is a test of anyone's nerve. Singing charms them, shouting frightens them – but it shouldn't be necessary to shoot them.

Leopard Seal – so called from its prominent spots, strong teeth, and active predation on penguins

Weddell Seal   *Leptonychotes weddelli*   (Lesson 1826)

SIZE   Males: nose-to-tail length 2.5–3 m: weight 250–400 kg. Females similar or slightly larger.

APPEARANCE   A dark grey seal with paler mottled flanks and silver-grey underparts, usually found lying fast asleep in the sun and snoring heavily. Teeth $\frac{2\ 1\ 3\ 2}{2\ 1\ 3\ 2}$; upper canines and large outer incisors prominent, often worn and damaged by ice; first and fifth cheek teeth smaller than the rest.

RANGE   A breeding species of inshore sea ice of the Antarctic continent and Peninsula, breeding also at the South Orkney, South Shetland and South Sandwich Islands: there is a tiny but stable breeding colony of up to a hundred on South Georgia. Vagrant in New Zealand, southern Australia and South America.

Weddell Seals are the common seals of inshore Antarctic ice, non-migratory and seldom seen out of sight of land. On fine days they sun themselves on the sea ice; from the air you can see them scattered singly or in small groups, lying close to the cracks through which they dive for food. In the dim twilight below the ice they hunt fish and squid. Their eyes are large and adapted for low light intensities. They dive deep – to 600 m and more – and may stay below for over an hour. Strange, trilling canary-like calls, audible at the surface, help them to locate fish in deep water and find their way back to their holes in the ice far above. In cold weather they stay permanently in the water, keeping the breathing holes open by rasping the ice with their teeth. The front teeth are also used for cutting steps in the ice; perhaps not surprisingly they are often badly worn and broken. In spring mature male Weddell Seals dominate the breathing holes, fighting each other for possession under water and keeping the younger males away. Pregnant cows gather at the holes in September and October, giving birth on the ice. The pups, over a metre long, change from their pale grey natal down to their dark juvenile coat at three to four weeks, and swim soon afterwards. Courtship and mating occur in the water in November and December. Weddell Seals have few natural enemies and only occasionally meet man. World population, hard to estimate, lies between 250,000 and 400,000.

Weddell Seals are the friendly seals of the Antarctic, well known to polar explorers and scientists who work and travel over the inshore sea ice. Soon after the sun returns in spring, the Weddell Seals make their appearance; though probably present through the winter, they emerge only when the air is warm enough and the sun bright enough for basking. They sleep soundly; creep up quietly and you can take their skin temperature, monitor their breathing rate and heart-beat, count their bristles and even paint an identifying patch on their flank without waking them. Lie alongside and they take you for another seal; stand upright and they watch you warily for a time – but usually go back to sleep in the end. Only a mother with pup may be aggressive, both to scientists and to other seals.

48

Weddell Seal

Weddell Seal. An inshore species of Antarctica that hunts its prey – mostly fish – under the sea ice. Eyes and jaws of this species (*below, left*) are relatively larger than those of the squid-eating Ross Seal (*below, right*)

Weddell Seal   Ross Seal

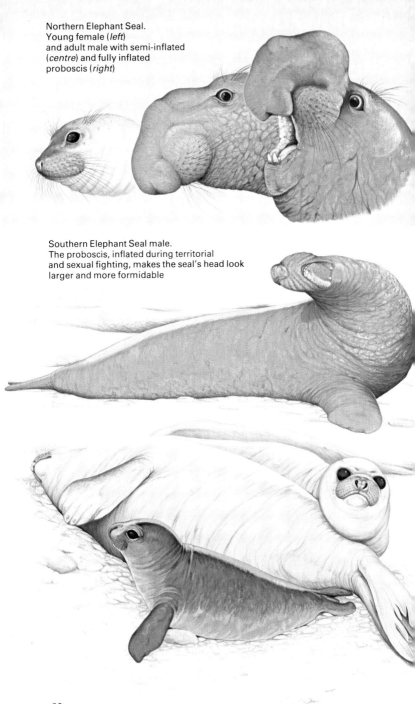

Northern Elephant Seal.
Young female (*left*)
and adult male with semi-inflated
(*centre*) and fully inflated
proboscis (*right*)

Southern Elephant Seal male.
The proboscis, inflated during territorial
and sexual fighting, makes the seal's head look
larger and more formidable

50

Northern Elephant Seal   *Mirounga angustirostris*   (Gill 1866)

SIZE   Males: nose-to-tail length 5–6.5 m; weight of large adults 3–4 tonnes. Females much smaller, 3–4 m long and weighing up to 1 tonne.

APPEARANCE   A very large elephant-grey seal, similar to its southern counterpart, perhaps marginally smaller. Mature males have a pendulous trunk overhanging the mouth, inflated in threat and used in producing the resonant calls. Teeth $\frac{2\ 1\ 4\ 1}{1\ 1\ 4\ 1}$; canines large, cheek teeth small and peg-like.

RANGE   Breeds on islands off southern California and Baja California, ranging to near-by islands and, more rarely, to coastal islands as far north as Alaska.

Northern Elephant Seals are absent from their island haunts in autumn and early winter. Mature males haul out in December, while the weather is still cool. The most dominant ones take up beach sites, where they are joined by females emerging from the sea; throughout January and February they form small, shifting harems of up to a dozen cows from which other males are excluded. The pups, born between January and March, wear dark woolly down for six to eight weeks; the mothers feed them for a month, and swim with them in the surf during the final stages of lactation and weaning. Mating occurs in January and February, and the adults haul out again to moult in late spring and summer. This species was hunted almost to extinction during the nineteenth century, leaving a remnant breeding population of reputedly no more than twenty by the early 1890s. Under protection the population has now increased to an estimated 30,000 or more.

Southern Elephant Seal   *Mirounga leonina*   (Linnaeus 1758)

SIZE   Males: nose-to-tail length 5–6.5 m: weight probably up to 4 tonnes. Females much smaller, 3–4 m long and weighing up to 1 tonne.

APPEARANCE   A monstrous grey-brown seal. Fully grown males are enormous, with a short pendulous trunk inflatable to football size during the breeding season. Old males are almost hairless, and heavily scarred on head and shoulders from fighting. Females and sub-adult males have coarse blue-grey to brown fur. Teeth $\frac{2\ 1\ 4\ 1}{1\ 1\ 4\ 1}$; the canines are large and deep-rooted, the cheek teeth small and peg-like.

RANGE   The Southern Ocean, breeding on southern Argentina, Tierra del Fuego and most of the cold temperate and sub-Antarctic islands. Immature animals range south to Antarctic shores, and north to New Zealand, Australia and South Africa, where lone females occasionally give birth to pups.

Southern Elephant Seals, largest of all living species of seal, spend much of the winter at sea. They feed on fish and squid, caught mainly in deep water. In spring (September) they haul out on to the beaches of their southern islands, a few on to sea ice. Mature males arrive first, staking out their claims to territories with much noisy fighting and threat display. The inflated trunk figures prominently as a visual threat; it also forms an echo chamber with the

Northern Elephant Seal. Females and pup. Females crowd together with their pups in the harems (*below*)

Southern Elephant Seal. Immature male. Northern and southern forms are very similar, but probably never meet in the wild

mouth, producing roars of elephantine sonority. The pregnant females follow, forming large, indeterminate groups from which the dominant males try constantly to exclude their rivals. Pups are born about a week after their mothers arrive. Over a metre long and clad in black wool, they feed ravenously on the rich milk, trebling or quadrupling their birth weight of 45 kg within three weeks. Mating occurs as the pups are weaned, and the cows return to sea. At five weeks the pups, now with sleek grey coats, also leave the beaches, and the exhausted bulls give up their territories. Through midsummer the adults fatten at sea, then return to moult. They spend over a month ashore, packed like sardines in foul-smelling wallows, sleeping, quarrelling, and shedding their fur in strips, and then slip away to sea as the cold weather approaches. Males are mature enough to hold territories from about their tenth year, sometimes earlier; females breed from their third year. Southern Elephant Seals were hunted almost to extinction for their oil during the nineteenth and early twentieth centuries, but are now almost completely protected at all their breeding sites. World population probably exceeds 600,000.

SUPERFAMILY OTARIOIDEA

Eared or otarioid seals fall into two families – Otariidae containing the fur seals and sea lions, and Odobenidae including only the walruses. In otarioids the hind flippers turn forward and the fore-flippers are long and bent. Both pairs of limbs can be flexed under the raised body, and the flippers have black leather soles instead of fur on their undersides. Nails are prominent on some of the toes, usually well back from the trailing edges. Fur seals and sea lions walk or run with limbs tucked under the body; walruses might, but are usually too fat and lazy to bother.

FAMILY OTARIIDAE

In the family Otariidae the fur seals and sea lions have small ear pinnae and a short free tail, and the males have scrotal testes. With less blubber than either phocides or walruses they are more lively and alert, with longer, more flexible necks and dog-like heads. In slow swimming they row with fore-flippers extended; swimming fast they use the flexible hind flippers and pelvic region as a propellor.

Fur seals and sea lions look like huge, misshapen dogs, with heavy shoulders and a sleek tapering body. The feet, flattened and enormously extended, splay out sideways as they walk. Mature males, always longer than their mates, have a matted, lion-like mane. Tiny pointed ears stick up prominently. The snout is square-cut and bristled; the eyes are dark, and well-glazed with secretions that overflow and streak down the face. Sea lions are generally larger and more heavily built than fur seals. Their fur is single-layered, lacking the velvety underpile that gives fur-seal pelts their commercial value.

Fur seals form the subfamily Arctocephalinae, sea lions the subfamily Otariinae; the two have similar Pacific and Southern Ocean distributions, often breeding close to each other in neighbouring colonies.

FAMILY OTARIIDAE

Subfamily Arctocephalinae

Arctocephalus australis (3 races)	South American Fur Seal
Arctocephalus doriferus (2 races)	Australian Fur Seal
Arctocephalus forsteri	New Zealand Fur Seal
Arctocephalus philippii (2 races)	Guadalupe Fur Seal
Arctocephalus pusillus	South African Fur Seal
Arctocephalus tropicalis (2 races)	Kerguelen Fur Seal
Callorhinus ursinus	Northern Fur Seal

Subfamily Otariinae

Otaria byronia	South American Sea Lion
Eumetopias jubata	Steller's Sea Lion
Zalophus californianus (3 races)	Californian Sea Lion
Neophoca cinerea	Australian Sea Lion
Phocarctos hookeri	Hooker's (New Zealand) Sea Lion

53

SUBFAMILY ARCTOCEPHALINAE

Fur seals originated in northern cool temperate waters of the Pacific Ocean, where they are still represented by one species. They seem to have spread southwards, possibly along the eastern Pacific corridor of cool surface waters, and invaded the southern warm-and-cool-temperate zones, forming a complex of closely related species and subspecies ranging from Guadalupe (Mexico) to islands of the Antarctic fringe. Their current pattern of distribution may have been complicated by nineteenth-century hunting; some breeding grounds probably lost their original stocks altogether, gaining new and perhaps different species during the recent resurgence of populations. Generally smaller than sea lions, they are distinguished by their more sharply pointed noses and dense, velvety underfur, part-hidden in the living animal by coarse outer guard hairs. On the fore-flippers the thumb is shorter than the second digit; the hind flippers are square-cut with all the toes of equal length (cf. Otariinae).

Northern Fur Seal   *Callorhinus ursinus*   (Linnaeus 1758)

SIZE   Males: nose-to-tail length 2–2.3 m, weighing up to 270 kg. Females to 1.6 m, weighing up to 65 kg.

APPEARANCE   Males dark chestnut brown, grizzled about the mane, with paler chest. Females dark grey-brown dorsally, paler underneath, with brown underfur. Teeth $\frac{3\;1\;3\;3}{2\;1\;3\;2}$; cheek teeth well-spaced pegs.

RANGE   Main breeding sites are on the Pribilov and Commander Islands in the Bering Sea, and Robben Island in the southern Sea of Okhotsk; during offshore winter migrations herds travel south to central Japanese waters in the west and southern California in the east.

Biologically the best known of any species of seal, the Northern Fur Seal has been 'managed' since 1910–11, when its heavily hunted and declined stocks were made the subject of an international agreement. Previously open to killing both on the breeding colonies and on migration, it was protected at sea and subject to controlled culling of young bulls, within limited periods, on land. Under management, stocks are estimated to have increased to about 1.5 million, while over 3 million skins have been taken. The herds may currently be expanding: a new colony is reported to have become established recently on a Californian island.

The herds return to their rocky shore breeding colonies in early June; harem bulls establish territories and collect forty to fifty pregnant cows about them. Most pups are born between mid-June and mid-July; about 70 cm long and shiny black, they look and sound like cross Labrador puppies. They are suckled for about a week, then left in crèches by their mothers who – newly mated – go back to sea. The mothers return every few days, call out their own pups from the noisy, boisterous crowd, and feed them. The pups grow slowly, playing together over the rocks and occasionally in the sea. At about two months they acquire a fine grey and white coat; after three months they leave for the sea. Adults undergo their annual moult about this time, and the herds leave in small groups for their southern migration from September onwards. Northern Fur Seals feed on fish and squid, and are reported to dive to 100 m and deeper after them.

Male Northern Fur Seals. A species of the sub-Arctic Pacific islands. It has flourished under a rational management programme

South American Fur Seal   *Arctocephalus australis*   (Zimmermann 1783)

SIZE   Males: nose-to-tail length 1.8–2 m, weight to 135 kg. Females: 1.5 m, 40 kg. Those of the Falkland Islands tend to be largest; Galapagos Islands seals are smallest, with the sexes more similar.

APPEARANCE   Males dark grey with a prominent mane of longer, paler fur about the neck and shoulders; underparts yellow, flippers reddish-brown. Females more uniformly grey-brown. Teeth $\frac{3\ 1\ 3\ 3}{2\ 1\ 3\ 2}$; cheek teeth small with sharp cusps.

RANGE   Three races are identified: (i) *A.a. australis* on the Falkland islands only; (ii) *A.a. gracilis* on southern South America, their colonies distributed patchily on islands of southern Brazil, Uruguay, Argentina and Chile and northward (very sparsely) to southern Peru along the west coast; (iii) *A.a. galapagoensis* on the Galapagos Islands only.

South American Fur Seals of the mainland and Falkland Islands congregate typically on their breeding grounds during November, the mature bulls taking up their territorial positions early in the month, and the females emerging later to gather about them in small harems of two or three. Most of the pups are born in November and December. Galapagos Islands stocks have a longer, possibly unlimited breeding season. This species is exploited commercially on several Uruguayan islands. Elsewhere it is protected, though poaching may be keeping numbers down in other breeding localities. There are estimated to be about 20,000 of the Falkland Islands race in six or seven major colonies, possibly 75,000 to 100,000 of the mainland race, mostly in Uruguay, Argentina and southern Chile, and 1,000 to 2,000 in scattered colonies of the Galapagos Islands.

Australian Fur Seal   *Arctocephalus doriferus*   (Wood Jones 1925)

SIZE   Males: nose-to-tail length 2.3–2.6 m; weight up to 360 kg. Females: 1.5–1.7 m; weight up to about 100 kg.

APPEARANCE   A large, dusty grey-brown seal, dark dorsally and paler underneath. Teeth $\frac{3\ 1\ 3\ 3}{2\ 1\ 3\ 2}$.

RANGE   Restricted to Tasmania and the south-eastern corner of Australia from Lady Julia Percy Island to Sydney, gathering mainly on offshore islands.

Australian Fur Seal. A grey-brown seal of south-eastern Australian waters

South American Fur Seal male. Stocks are now recovering from heavy hunting in the nineteenth century

This seal is similar in several respects to the South African Fur Seal, and regarded by some taxonomists as subspecifically related. Little is known of its biology. Breeding occurs in November and December, peaking about a month earlier than in New Zealand Fur Seals of south-western Australia; despite their geographical closeness, contacts between the two species are only rarely recorded.

Australian Fur Seal

South African Fur Seal. It is found on islands off the southern African coast; controlled hunting yields many thousands of skins yearly

South African Fur Seal   *Arctocephalus pusillus*   (Schreber 1776)

SIZE   Males: nose-to-tail length 2.1–2.4 m, weight over 300 kg in full fat. Females up to 2 m long, weighing up to 130 kg.

APPEARANCE   Dark grey seals, slate-coloured above and paler on the chest and belly. Teeth $\frac{3\;1\;3\;3}{2\;1\;3\;2}$.

RANGE   South-western and southern coasts of Africa, from Cape Cross, Namibia (22°S) to Bird Island, South Africa (27°E); breeding in over twenty colonies, mostly on inshore rocky islets.

One of the larger fur seals – perhaps the largest of all – this species has been exploited commercially for several centuries, under licence for more than a century. The annual cycle starts in November when the harems form. Pups are born in late November and early December, and mating follows within a week. During late summer and autumn mothers may leave their pups for several days together. By April and May most of the pups have moulted into their sub-adult grey-brown fur: they accompany their mothers to sea and catch fish and crustaceans, but may supplement their diet with milk for several months further. The best pelts come from pups six to eight months old, taken from the colonies in winter; young non-breeding males have also been taken during an early summer cull. South African Fur Seals feed mainly on small surface-living fish, crustaceans and cephalopods. The total population is estimated at over 500,000.

Kerguelen Fur Seal *Arctocephalus tropicalis* (Peters 1872)

SIZE   Males: nose-to-tail length 1.6–2.0 m, weight about 120 kg. Females: 1.4–1.6 m, weight 40–50 kg.

APPEARANCE   Small, dog-like seals, usually lively and alert, with predominantly grey upper parts fading to brown; dark head, shoulders and flippers, yellow or creamy-brown face and chest. The northern race tends to be greyer than the southern. Mature males have a crest and cape of long fur on head and shoulders. Teeth $\frac{3\,1\,3\,3}{2\,1\,3\,2}$; cheek teeth thin spikes; cusps tiny or absent.

RANGE   Breeds on islands in the southern Atlantic, Indian and Southern Oceans from longitude 60°W to 80°E. There are two geographical races, living respectively north and south of the Antarctic Convergence: (i) *A.t tropicalis* occurs on Tristan da Cunha, Gough Island, Marion and Prince Edward Islands, and Îles Crozet, Amsterdam and St Paul; (ii) *A.t. gazella* occurs on the South Shetland, South Orkney and South Sandwich Islands, South Georgia, Bouvetøya, Îles Kerguelen and Heard Island. Vagrants have been reported far to the east on Macquarie Island, and possibly on New Zealand.

These lively little animals, almost exterminated by nineteenth-century sealing gangs, have made a remarkable recovery – slow at first, but currently explosive. Rarely seen during the 1920s, they are now breeding again in most of their old haunts. Some Antarctic islands have been re-colonized in the last twenty to thirty years. Several – South Georgia, for example – have built up sizeable populations numbering tens of thousands in the same period. Though not yet exploited commercially on a large scale, some of these stocks may be subject to poaching. The total population probably exceeds 100,000, and growth seems to be continuing at every monitored breeding centre.

Kerguelen Fur Seal. Heavily hunted in the nineteenth century, its stocks are making a spectacular recovery on many southern islands

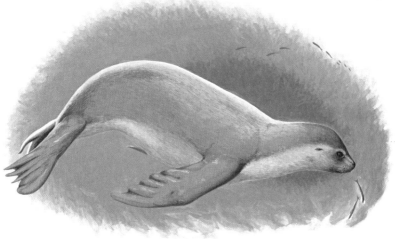

Guadalupe Fur Seal *Arctocephalus philippii* (Peters 1866)

SIZE   Males: nose-to-tail length about 2 m, weight about 130 kg. Females: about 1.5 m, weight probably 40–50 kg.

APPEARANCE   Similar to the South American Fur Seal. Teeth $\frac{3\ 1\ 3\ 3}{2\ 1\ 3\ 2}$.

RANGE   There are two races, restricted mainly to two small and widely spaced island groups: (i) *A.p. philippii* on Juan Fernandez Island (south-eastern Pacific Ocean) and (ii) *A.p. townsendi* of Guadalupe Island (off Baja California), an occasional visitor to nearby islands and the mainland coast.

This species was first identified on Juan Fernandez Island, off the coast of Chile, in 1866; though similar to the South American Fur Seal, it has a distinctly narrower skull. The same characteristic was later found in skulls of seals butchered on Guadalupe Island, off the Mexican coast, and the two stocks were linked as a single species. Discovered at a time when both were on the point of extinction, their biology was never closely studied, and by the turn of the century it seemed likely that neither had survived. However, both have now recovered. A few were found breeding on Guadalupe in 1927, and the population there now numbers several thousand. Juan Fernandez too has recovered its indigenous race; colonies totalling several hundred were reported in 1969 and 1970. San Ambrosio, one of a group of islands 1,100 km north of Juan Fernandez, may also be acquiring a small stock. Like their South American neighbours, these tropical fur seals breed communally, the cows forming small harems about the mature bulls; pupping and mating occur, however, in May and June. The colonies form among tumbled rocks and in caves at sea level, where the breeding adults and pups seek shelter from the hot midday sun. These small island stocks, though protected by Chilean and Mexican law, are very much at risk from poaching, disturbance and epidemic diseases.

New Zealand Fur Seal. Closely related to the Australian Fur Seal, this species is restricted to southern New Zealand and offshore islands

New Zealand Fur Seal *Arctocephalus forsteri* (Lesson 1828)

SIZE Males: nose-to-tail length 2–2.3 m, weight to about 180 kg. Females: 1.8–2 m, weight to about 80 kg.

APPEARANCE Back and flanks smoky grey, fading to dusty brown; underparts paler. Teeth $\frac{3\ 1\ 3\ 3}{2\ 1\ 3\ 2}$; cheek teeth broad, with small but prominent lateral cusps.

RANGE Widespread on scattered headlands about New Zealand's South Island and Stewart Island, breeding on Open Bay, Snares and other islands of southern New Zealand, and on Chatham, Bounty, Campbell, Macquarie and possibly other cold temperate islands. The same species breeds also on islands of the south-western Australian coast from Eclipse Island to Kangaroo Island.

Protected in New Zealand almost continuously since 1916, and virtually ignored by all but hostile fishermen in Australia, the species has increased its numbers steadily over several decades. Recent studies show that the breeding colonies are occupied for most of the year. Harems form from early November, most pups are born in December, and many of the pups still remain in the colonies nine or ten months later when the mature bulls begin to take up their breeding sites again. Total population probably exceeds 60,000 and continues to expand slowly.

Guadalupe Fur Seal, a species found on Juan Fernandez Island (Chile) and Guadalupe, off Baja California

SUBFAMILY OTARIINAE

The sea lions, like the fur seals, are believed to have originated in the northern Pacific Ocean and spread southward into the temperate and cool areas of the southern hemisphere. Like the fur seals (which they strongly resemble) they are only rarely seen as vagrants in the Arctic, and have never managed to invade the north Atlantic Ocean. In the north Pacific, Steller's Sea Lion is the cool temperate and subpolar species, patchily distributed in an arc from northern Japan to northern California. The Californian Sea Lion prefers the warmer waters of southern Japan, southern and Baja California and the Galapagos Islands – three isolated localities where subspecies have developed. The three southern hemisphere forms in Australia, New Zealand and South America are usually given full species – even full generic – status. Sea lions have the first digit of the fore-flipper longer than the inner. Their fur is coarse, without a dense silky underfur. Where sea lions and fur seals share an environment (as they often do), sea lions usually select open beaches sheltered from heavy surf. They tend to breed slightly later than neighbouring fur seals, and feed closer inshore.

South American Sea Lion. A small species of the temperate South American islands

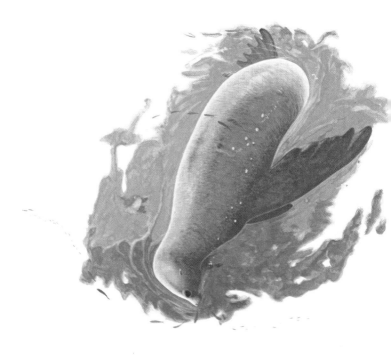

South American Sea Lion   *Otaria byronia*   (Blainville 1820)

SIZE   Males: head-to-tail length 2.8 m, weight to 300 kg. Females: up to 2 m long, weighing 60 kg.

APPEARANCE   Dark brown back, fading to dull tan in summer; yellow-brown underparts. Males develop a shaggy brown or yellow mane over the head and shoulders; females, altogether smaller and more slender, have no mane but the head and neck are paler than the rest of the body. Pups are born black or dark brown, moulting to grey after a few months; yearlings are reddish-brown. Teeth $\frac{3\ 1\ 4\ 2}{2\ 1\ 4\ 1}$; the last upper molar is often lost.

RANGE   Southern South America, from about 12°S in Brazil to Uruguay, the Falkland Islands, Argentina, Tierra del Fuego, Chile, and Peru to 4°S. Breeding range uncertain; on the east coast most colonies lie south of 30°S, but in the west scattered breeding groups extend northward to the Peruvian Chincha Islands (11°S) and possibly beyond.

These are large, heavily built sea lions that live gregariously on beaches and flat ground within a few hundred metres of the sea. They are best known from studies in the Falkland Islands, where they are present throughout the year, spending much of their time in the water but coming ashore to sleep in untidy heaps. In spring the large bulls take up closely spaced breeding territories along the beaches, rounding up harems of eight to ten mature females and fighting off rivals. Pups are born in summer, mostly in late December and early January. Mating occurs a few days after the birth of the pups. The pups may be fed for up to a year or even longer, though most have begun to hunt for themselves by the time they are six months old. Hunting has driven some stocks of South American Sea Lions to living on inaccessible shores where their mortality is high. Elsewhere stocks have declined mysteriously. Those on the Falkland Islands seem to have fallen from over 300,000 estimated in the 1930s to no more than 30,000 today – and nobody knows why. But this is a plentiful species; world population stands at about 275,000.

Steller's Sea Lion   *Eumetopias jubata*   (Schreber 1776)

SIZE   Male: nose-to-tail length 3.7 m, weight up to 1 tonne. Females up to 2.6 m, weighing up to 270 kg.

APPEARANCE   Large, yellowish brown; males ponderous, with a shaggy shoulder-length mane, females much smaller and maneless. Pups are born dark brown and remain dark through their first year. Teeth $\frac{3\ 1\ 5}{2\ 1\ 5}$; cheek teeth peg-like, with a wide gap between 4 and 5.

RANGE   Northern Pacific Ocean coasts and islands, from Hokkaido to the Bering Sea and south to southern California. Breeds on eastern Sakhalin Island in the northern Sea of Okhotsk, eastern Kamchatka, the Pribilov and Aleutian Islands, Kodiak Island, many islands off south-eastern Alaska and British Columbia, and the Santa Barbara Islands off California. They have been reported as far south as Korea, and one is reported to have visited Herschel Island in the Arctic Ocean.

This is an abundant species, successful over a wide geographical range from subtropical California to the polar ocean. Like most other sea lions, however, Steller's Sea Lions prefer temperate climates to extremes; their main centre of

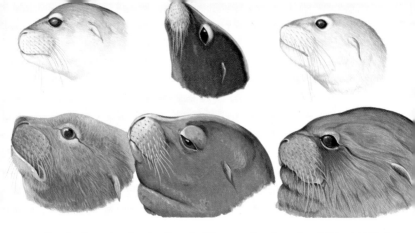

Females (*upper*) and males (*lower*) of three species of sea lion; left to right Steller's (Northern), Californian, New Zealand

breeding is the chilly Aleutian Islands, where possibly more than one third of the world's population of 200,000 to 300,000 is concentrated. Breeding starts in May, when bulls take up their beach territories and establish harems of up to twenty cows. Pups are born in late May and June, and mating occurs soon afterwards. The pups enter the water at four to six weeks, but are fed on mother's milk for at least three months, often longer. Adults feed on squid and a wide range of fish, competing with fishermen in their home waters. Their populations are controlled locally rather than exploited; the skin is unbeautiful (except on a sea lion) but useful for patching boats and tanning to make tough leather.

Californian Sea Lion   *Zalophus californianus*   (Lesson 1828)

SIZE   Males: nose-to-tail 2–2.5 m, weighing up to 300 kg. Females smaller, up to 2 m long and weighing up to 100 kg.

APPEARANCE   Typically dark grey-brown to black, with some local variation; Japanese and Galapagos Islands stocks may be paler. Mature males have little mane, but thick, muscular forequarters and a high domed forehead; females and immature males are slender, even svelte, without trace of a mane. Teeth $\frac{3}{2}\frac{1}{1}\frac{5}{5}$ or 6, peg-like.

RANGE   Three geographical races are identified, with widely differing ranges: (i) *Z.c. californianus*, Vancouver Island to Islas Tres Marias, breeding on many small offshore islands of California and the Sonoran coast of Mexico; (ii) *Z.c. japonicus*, islands on the Sea of Japan; (iii) *Z.c. wollebaeki*, Galapagos Islands only.

A small, lively sea lion with curiously disjunct distribution. Well-mannered and biddable in captivity, especially when young, this is the species most likely to be presented as a 'performing seal' in a circus. Despite their wide scattering, the three races are remarkably similar; it is difficult to tell their skulls apart, though those from Galapagos tend to be smaller and more slender than others. The best-known race is that from California, where it has been studied on land and in the water. Breeding beaches, occupied haphazardly for much of the year, are brought to order with the start of breeding in May. The big mature bulls space themselves out and gather sprawling harems of up to a dozen females about them. Bulls roar defiance at each other across invisible territory boundaries, and the cows squabble among themselves. Into this mêlée the pups are born, mostly in June; dark brown at birth, they soon add their bawling cries (by which their mothers identify them) to the general noise. The parents mate again two weeks after birth. Bulls disperse after mating; mothers suckle their young for several weeks, taking them to sea at intervals from the first two or three weeks onwards. Some remain together for a year or more. Fish and squid are the main diet; large animals in captivity thrive on about 6 kg of fish per day. There are probably over 50,000 of these sea lions in California and 20,000 in the Galapagos, but only a few hundred in Japanese waters.

Steller's Sea Lion, widespread in the northern Pacific Ocean from Japan to California

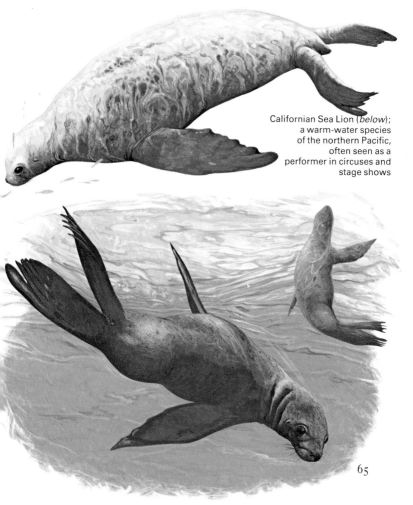

Californian Sea Lion (*below*); a warm-water species of the northern Pacific, often seen as a performer in circuses and stage shows

65

Australian Sea Lion *Neophoca cinerea* (Péron 1816)

SIZE   Males: nose-to-tail length 3.5–4.2 m, weight unknown. Females smaller and more slender, up to 1.8 m long and weighing 63–100 kg.
APPEARANCE   Males large and stocky; silver-grey to sandy brown all over, with grizzled yellow mane. Females dark grey or brown dorsally, paler underneath, more slenderly built. Teeth $\frac{3\ 1\ 5}{2\ 1\ 5}$; cheek teeth peg-like.
RANGE   Restricted to the west coast of Australia (Houtman's Abrolhos and nearby islands) and southern Australia from Eclipse Island (near Albany) and the Recherche Archipelago to Kangaroo Island.

Like caricature Aussies of popular fiction, Australian Sea Lions are large, lively and quarrelsome, always ready for a fight, and with hides tough enough for boot leather. Formerly widespread along the coast, they are now restricted to little-used offshore islands. Once they were hunted for their meat and oil. Now of little commercial interest, they are mostly allowed to live and breed in peace; only the local fishermen dispute with them from time to time over damage to fish-stocks and nets. They live close to the breeding beaches throughout the year. Bulls take up breeding territories in October and gather small groups of four to six pregnant cows about them. Both sexes quarrel with neighbours and each other. The dark brown pups are born in late November and December. Large and well developed at birth, they play together in groups when only a few days old, swim in shallow pools at one to two weeks, and venture into the sea with their mothers before they are three months old. Australian Sea Lions seem permanently aggressive towards each other, and the pups grow up in an unfriendly world where any juvenile, and almost any adult except their mother, will savage them unmercifully on the least provocation. The total population is about 5,000 to 10,000.

Hooker's (New Zealand) Sea Lion *Phocarctos hookeri* (Gray 1866)

SIZE   Males: nose-to-tail length 3–3.4 m, weights unknown. Females much smaller, seldom exceeding 2 m.
APPEARANCE   Medium-sized dark brown, reddish or tan sea lions; mature males usually darker with mahogany brown mane, females sandy or yellowish. Teeth $\frac{3\ 1\ 5}{2\ 1\ 5}$.
RANGE   Breeds on islands south of New Zealand, notably Enderby Island of the Auckland Islands group, and Campbell Island further south. Non-breeding animals appear on Macquarie Island, the Snares Islands and southern New Zealand.

Akin to Australian Sea Lions (some authors include both in the same genus), Hooker's Sea Lions are smaller animals with a gentler disposition and a tendency to pack closely together for warmth. Bulls appear on the breeding beaches of their island homes in October. The cows follow in November and December, forming small harem groups which the dominant males adopt and defend against rivals; aggressive posturing, roaring and fighting keep the younger bulls at bay. Pups are born from December onward, and mating of the adults follows soon after. In the late summer the harems break up; the bulls disperse, and the cows wander off to sea, returning at intervals through autumn and winter to feed their slowly growing pups. Heavily hunted for oil and skins in the nineteenth century, Hooker's Sea Lion stocks are still recovering; the total population may now have reached 50,000.

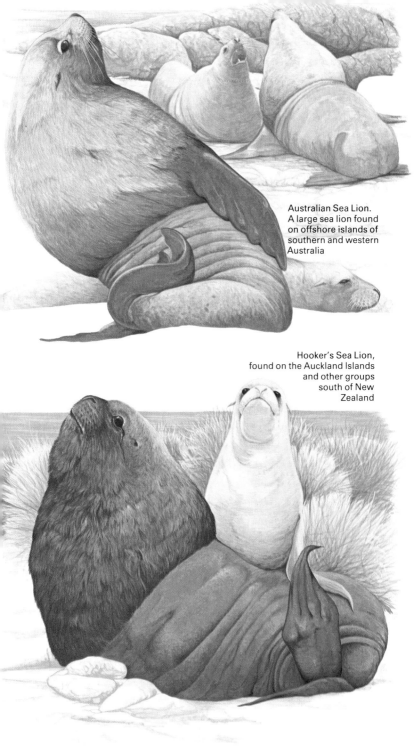

Australian Sea Lion.
A large sea lion found
on offshore islands of
southern and western
Australia

Hooker's Sea Lion,
found on the Auckland Islands
and other groups
south of New
Zealand

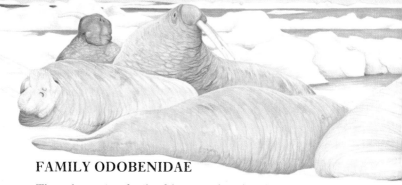

FAMILY ODOBENIDAE

The walruses, in a family of their own, have lost their ear pinnae and much of their fur. Their most striking features are their massive bulk, bristling moustaches and the huge canine tusks that they use for raking the sea bed in search of clams, their favourite food. There is only one species, circumpolar in Arctic and sub-Arctic waters.

FAMILY ODOBENIDAE

Odobenus rosmarus   Walrus

Walrus   *Odobenus rosmarus*   (Linnaeus 1758)

SIZE   Males: nose-to-tail length 3–3.7 m, weight up to 1.5 tonnes. Females slightly shorter and 30–40 per cent lighter in weight.
APPEARANCE   Like huge, overgrown sea lions, Walruses are the otariid equivalent of elephant seals, and second only to them in size. Thick, almost hairless brown hide (wrinkled even in newborn pups); broad, blunt head with tiny eyes, and external ears barely visible. The upper lips, enormously padded, bristle like pincushions with sensory hairs. Teeth $\frac{1\ 1\ 3\ 0}{0\ 1\ 3\ 0}$; the upper canines form prominent tusks in both sexes; the cheek teeth are flattened and reduced.
RANGE   There are two very similar geographical races: (i) *O.r. rosmarus*, the Atlantic Walrus, found from northern and eastern Hudson Bay to Devon and Ellesmere Islands, Baffin Island and western Greenland, with smaller populations off northern Iceland and in the Kara and Barents Seas north beyond Franz Josef Land; (ii) *O.r. divergens*, the Pacific Walrus of the northern Bering, Chukchi, East Siberian and Laptev Seas; it is found mainly on inshore sea ice over shallow water. Vagrants have wandered as far south as Britain and Japan.

With their unwieldy bulk, wrinkles, piggy eyes and permanently aggrieved expressions, Walruses are perhaps the least beautiful of all the seals, though like others they acquire grace on entering the water. Highly gregarious, they gather in clubs on beaches and ice-floes, and swim in large herds during their seasonal movements as the sea ice advances and retreats. They feed on the sea bed, using their massive ivory tusks (up to a metre long in large males) to stir the mud in search of cockles, clams and molluscs; the sensitive bristles are probably important in food-finding, and the crushing teeth break open the shells. Walruses also take fish, and occasionally smaller seals. They gather on the fast ice in spring; the pups are born in April and May, and mating occurs soon after. Over 1 metre long at birth, and weighing more than 40 kg, the pups

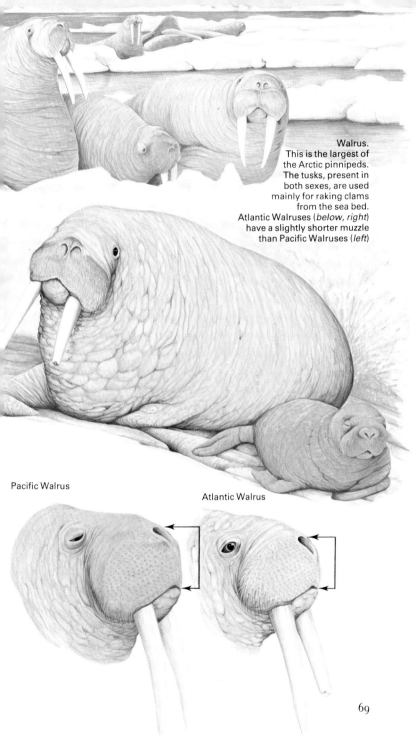

Walrus.
This is the largest of
the Arctic pinnipeds.
The tusks, present in
both sexes, are used
mainly for raking clams
from the sea bed.
Atlantic Walruses (*below, right*)
have a slightly shorter muzzle
than Pacific Walruses (*left*)

Pacific Walrus

Atlantic Walrus

69

grow slowly, quadrupling their birth weight during the first year. Gestation and lactation each last about twelve months, and females probably breed every third or fourth year. The two forms of Walrus are very similar; Pacific stocks have slightly broader faces and larger tusks. Hunting for oil, ivory and skins over two or three centuries has severely reduced them, and some local stocks (for example, those of the Laptev Sea) are small enough to cause concern. However, both subspecies are now largely protected, and total world population is probably between 100,000 and 150,000.

Sirenians – sea cows, dugongs and manatees

ORDER SIRENIA

Aquatic herbivorous mammals, the sirenians are distantly related to elephants and look like elephantine dolphins. They live in shallow seas, estuaries and rivers, feeding on sea grasses and other fixed or floating vegetation. Almost hairless, they are draped in leathery grey or brown hide. Fore-limbs are flippers; there are no hind limbs. The head is massive, without neck constriction; horny plates replace the incisors, and the remaining teeth, if present, are limited to small tusks or grinding molars. Sirenians mate and give birth in the water. They can haul their foreparts out to browse, but never emerge fully and are helpless on land. They have pectoral mammary glands and some are said to rest upright in the water supporting the feeding calf tenderly with one flipper. Rumour has it that seamen of old saw this posture at a distance and developed the mermaid legend to account for it. Anyone who has seen a homely sirenian at any distance – bald, bewhiskered, hare-lipped and lacking front teeth – finds this hard to believe. Formerly world-wide, there are now only two small families remaining, restricted respectively to tropical Indo-Pacific and Atlantic regions.

FAMILY DUGONGIDAE

The two species of this family differ enough to merit their own subfamilies. Steller's Sea Cows, enormous sirenians of the cold Bering Sea, were probably exterminated by hunting over two hundred years ago, though there are rumours of their living presence from time to time. Modern dugongs live in the warmer waters of the Indian and Pacific Oceans. Dugongs differ from manatees in having seven cervical vertebrae (manatees have six) and a less massive skeleton. Males have small tusk-like incisors that seldom show externally, and broad grinding cheek teeth. Their tail ends in two horizontal flukes, and the flippers are clawless.

FAMILY DUGONGIDAE

Subfamily Hydrodamalinae
Hydrodamalis gigas   Steller's Sea Cow
Subfamily Dugonginae
Dugong dugon   Dugong

Steller's Sea Cow   *Hydrodamalis gigas*   Zimmermann 1780

SIZE   Nose-to-tail length 9–11 m, greatest girth 8 m; weight (estimated) to about 24 tonnes.
APPEARANCE   Large grey-brown seal-like animals with rough, bark-like hide, fat-gutted but tapering rapidly towards the fluked tail. Teeth absent.
RANGE   Formerly abundant in coastal waters of the Bering and Copper Islands in the western Bering Sea; only vaguely reported elsewhere, though this species or closely related forms were probably widespread along northern Pacific coasts until destroyed by primitive man.

These huge beasts were probably familiar fare to earlier aboriginal populations of the north Pacific. Recorded for science in 1741, when a Russian expedition was wrecked in one of their few remaining habitats, they were described and studied by Georg Steller, the expedition doctor. They lived in shallow-water herds, browsing seaweeds. Buoyant with fat, their backs showed above the water as they fed, and the Russian seamen called them 'sea cows' – the name that all sirenians have since inherited. Unfortunately for the species their flesh proved highly palatable. Within thirty years of their discovery the total population of 1500 to 2000 was destroyed by sealers, who preferred their meat to that of the carnivorous sea mammals. Though the species is thought to have been exterminated, rumours of its survival persist down the years. Russian whalers working off Cape Navarin (north-western Bering Sea) in 1962 thought they saw half a dozen 6–8 m long in the water – but no breeding ground has yet been reported.

Steller's Sea Cow, a huge dugong of the northern Pacific, now almost certainly extinct

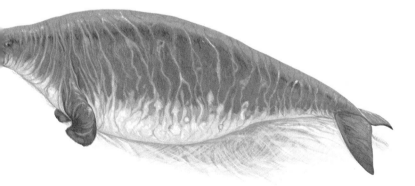

Dugong *Dugong dugon* (Müller 1776)

SIZE   Nose-to-tail length 3–4 m; sexes similar.

APPEARANCE   Seal-like animals with a tough, blue-grey hide, wrinkled and sparsely scattered with coarse hairs: sensory whiskers grow thick on the snout-like upper lip. Teeth $\frac{1\,0\,4}{0\,0\,4}$.

RANGE   Many island groups in the central and western Pacific Ocean, including Palou and the Caroline, Marshall and Solomon Islands; northern Australia, New Guinea, Indonesia, Malaysia, Taiwan, Ryukyu, Philippine Islands, Andaman Islands, India, Sri Lanka, Madagascar and eastern Africa, Kenya, Somalia and Red Sea coasts.

Dugongs appear in small, scattered populations over an immense area of the Indo-Pacific region. Entirely coastal (though clearly capable of travelling across open sea) they require only warm, silty shallows where sea-grasses and similar vegetation grow in abundance. They feed on the bottom; the disgruntled, down-turned mouth with its muscular lips and horny plates is well adapted for close browsing. Though often shy and present only in small numbers, large concentrations also are recorded, for example off the Horn of Africa and in northern Australia; Moreton Bay, near Brisbane, once held a herd almost 5 km long and 100 m wide. Heavy hunting has eliminated most of the big stocks, for dugongs, like other sirenians, provide very good meat, oil and hides. In Australia, where only aboriginals can kill them, dugongs are surviving best; recent research suggests that they breed in July and August, and that stocks are maintaining themselves adequately. Very little is known of their status elsewhere, but their vulnerability to hunters, palatability, slow rate of reproduction and the spread of hungry human populations into many of their haunts, give little promise for their future.

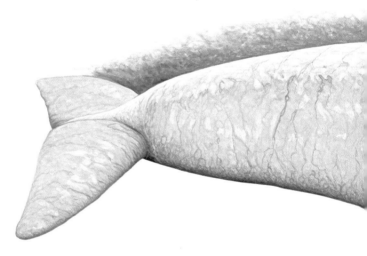

Dugong – placid browsers of tropical sea grasses, much in demand for their highly palatable 'beef'

FAMILY TRICHECHIDAE

Three species of manatees are alive today, all in warm waters of the Atlantic Ocean or the neighbouring rivers. Manatees have only six cervical vertebrae, and very heavy skeletons with ribs and skulls of massive proportions. Canines and incisors are missing; the grinding molars move forward and drop out when worn, to be replaced from behind. The tail is spade-shaped; the flippers are flat paddles tipped (in all but the Amazon River Manatees) with three fingernails.

FAMILY TRICHECHIDAE

Trichechus manatus (2 races)	Caribbean Manatee
Trichechus inunguis	South American River Manatee
Trichechus senegalensis	West African Manatee

Caribbean Manatee   *Trichechus manatus*   (Linnaeus 1758)

SIZE   Nose-to-tail length 3–4 m. Weight to 500 kg. Sexes similar.
APPEARANCE   A fat, dark-grey manatee, lighter underneath; leathery skin with sparse covering of hairs. Teeth $\frac{0\ 0\ 6–3}{0\ 0\ 6–8}$.
RANGE   Two geographical races: (i) *T.m. manatus*, West Indies and Caribbean coasts of Central and South America including the lower Orinoco River; (ii) *T.m. latirostris*, Florida; formerly on neighbouring coasts from North Carolina to Texas.

Normally solitary, Caribbean Manatees live in sheltered coastal waters, canals and rivers, browsing both under water and from overhanging banks. They are best known from Florida. Shyness tends to keep them away from the public, though a few have learned to trust snorkel divers and allow themselves to be patted. Several are killed each year by power boats; pollution and industrial development are growing hazards that restrict them to a few favoured localities. They breed at any time of the year. Cows and bulls come together only for a brief rutting period. Gestation lasts just over a year; the single calves (rarely twins), about 1 m long, are suckled for one or two years. Placid but vocal, manatees squeak and chirp to each other, and use their small, beady eyes in searching for food. A population of about a thousand is estimated for the Florida race. The Caribbean race is less favoured; though still plentiful, numbering several thousand, and legally protected in many parts of its range, it is widely hunted for meat and likely to be at risk before long.

West African Manatee   *Trichechus senegalensis*   (Link 1795)

SIZE   Not recorded; about the same as the Caribbean Manatee.
APPEARANCE   Not recorded.
RANGE   Coastal waters, lagoons and rivers of western Africa from Senegal to Angola, penetrating well inland.

Little is known of the biology of this species, which seems to resemble closely its American counterparts in form and ecology. Its range has decreased radically in recent years through hunting; populations are thin and at risk throughout its range.

South American River Manatee   *Trichechus inunguis*   (Natterer 1863)

SIZE   Not recorded; about the same as the Caribbean Manatee.
APPEARANCE   Similar to other manatees, but with a distinctive white patch on the chest, and long, nail-less flippers.
RANGE   Restricted to the rivers, lakes and estuary of the lower Amazon river basin.

A sea mammal only by courtesy, this is a freshwater species, formerly plentiful in the turbid rivers of Brazil, eastern Peru, Venezuela and Colombia, but now greatly reduced by hunting. Originally taken only by local Amer-indians, its fate was sealed when commercial hunters discovered its potential. Large numbers were killed and canned for export up to the late 1950s, when the remaining stocks of manatees and the industry finally collapsed together. Virtually nothing is known of the biology of this species, which is now very rare and – despite protective legislation – seriously in danger of extinction.

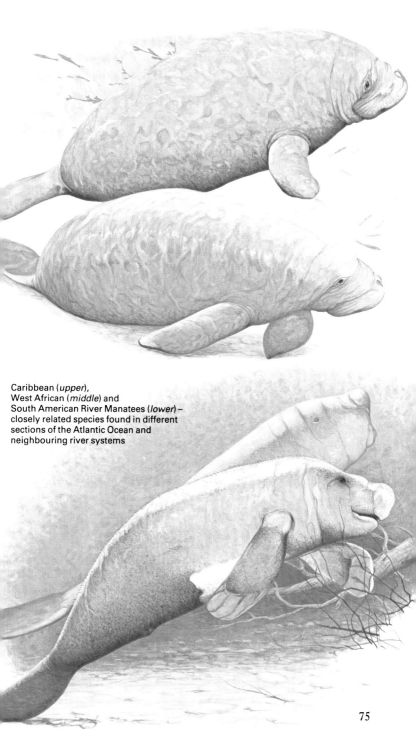

Caribbean (*upper*),
West African (*middle*) and
South American River Manatees (*lower*) –
closely related species found in different
sections of the Atlantic Ocean and
neighbouring river systems

Whales, porpoises and dolphins

ORDER CETACEA

Described by one distinguished zoologist as 'the most peculiar and aberrant of mammals', whales and their kin have evolved all the way towards aquatic living; they are entirely adapted for life in water, and cannot survive long if washed ashore. Most live in the open ocean, well away from land and its dangers. Some live inshore or enter sheltered waters to court or produce their calves. A few of the smaller species live in estuaries, fewer still in big rivers and lakes without access to the sea.

The biggest whales are enormous – 30 m long and weighing over 120 tonnes. But these are exceptional; only one species, the Blue Whale, has individuals that sometimes reach this size. The mean length of Blue Whales is probably closer to 25 m, their mean weight about 100 tonnes – roughly as long as five elephants in procession and as heavy as twenty. Any cetacean more than 10 m long tends to be called a whale, though it is a mark of respect rather than a scientific distinction. Mysticetes (of all sizes), sperm whales and beaked whales are the unequivocal true whales; all the rest – even the killer whales and pilot whales – are just big or smaller dolphins. Note that 'dolphin' is used in many senses. Some biologists like to reserve it for species of the family Delphinidae, but theirs is a losing battle. People generally use the term for practically any cetacean too small to call a whale, and that is how I use it here.

Living whales fall readily into two suborders, Odontoceti (the toothed whales) and Mysticeti (the baleen or whalebone whales); some zoologists regard these groups as entirely separate, derived from distinct non-whale ancestors and superficially similar only because the sea – a highly demanding medium – has worked on them in similar ways.

SUBORDER ODONTOCETI

This is the larger and more diverse of the two suborders; there are about sixty-four species, here listed in seven families (some zoologists prefer ten or more). The toothed whales are best recognized by the *absence* of baleen plates (p. 13). Nearly all have functional teeth as adults, though never divisible into incisors, canines and molars. Some dolphins show as many as 120 teeth, some bottle-nosed whales as few as two, or even none that penetrate the gums. Their blow-hole is a single aperture, and the upper surface of the skull is slightly asymmetrical, as though twisted to the right. The ribs, especially the double-headed anterior ones, are strongly hinged to the vertebrae, and there are usually bones representing all five fingers in the flippers.

Four of the seven families are listed in superfamilies of their own; the three remaining ones are grouped together in the large superfamily Delphinoidea –

Humpback Whale with calf

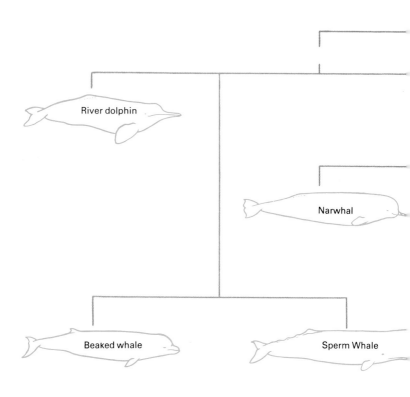

the true dolphins and porpoises. Toothed whales provide permanent headaches for taxonomists trying to name and classify them. Many species have been 'discovered' several times in different parts of the world and given several names, or described inadequately from sea-damaged specimens. The links that hold the families and genera together are tenuous, and no two classification systems are quite the same.

SUPERFAMILY PLATANISTOIDEA

FAMILY PLATANISTIDAE

This group includes only four species, the river or freshwater dolphins. They live widely scattered in South America and southern Asia. The species, each

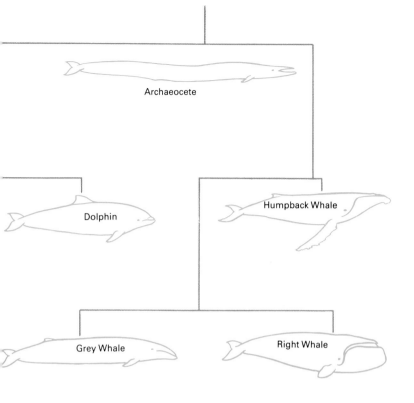

given a separate genus, share common anatomical peculiarities (for example, a distinct neck) that set them apart from the rest of the living Cetacea and link them with some of the oldest fossil groups of whales. Of more immediate interest to whale watchers is the fact that all live mainly or entirely in rivers and lakes, hence the group names of 'river dolphins' or 'freshwater dolphins'. However, they are not Delphinoid dolphins (p. 102) and they are not the only freshwater cetaceans: several species of real dolphins have found the big rivers and estuaries of the world very much to their liking, and often swim side by side with platanistoids.

Platanista and *Pontoporia* rate subfamilies of their own, on small points of skeletal anatomy; *Inia* and *Lipotes* share a third subfamily. All members of this family have separate and rather long cervicle vertebrae (hence the neck) and long narrow jaws with many sharp, fish-catching teeth. All four species have small eyes, which may be virtually useless to them in the muddy waters of estuaries. There is good evidence that some hunt mainly by sonar – sound echoes.

FAMILY PLATANISTIDAE

Subfamily Platanistinae
   Platanista gangetica   Indian River Dolphin (Susu)
Subfamily Iniinae
   Inia geoffrensis   Amazon River Dolphin
                                    (Boutu)
   Lipotes vexillifer   White Fin Dolphin (Beiji or
                                    Baijitun)
Subfamily Pontoporiinae
   Pontoporia blainvillei   La Plata River Dolphin
                                    (Franciscana)

Indian River Dolphin (Susu)   *Platanista gangetica*   Roxburgh 1801

SIZE   Nose-to-tail length 2–2.5 m. Sexes similar.

APPEARANCE   Dark or pale uniform grey; the flippers are square-cut and there is a
marked dorsal ridge, rising to a low, elongate dorsal fin. About 29 small sharp teeth in
each half-jaw.

RANGE   There are two closely similar races which some regard as species; (i) *P.g. indi*
of the Indus River and its tributaries, and *P.g. gangetica* of the Gunga (Ganges)
and Brahmaputra systems. Both are widespread in their respective rivers from the
Himalayan foothills to tidal waters.

This small dolphin is restricted to northern rivers of India. The tiny eyes
lack lenses; Susus live mainly in muddy water, hunting their prey (fish and
bottom-living crabs) by sonar. Formerly quite plentiful, they are now an
endangered species. The erection of dams and barriers across their rivers
(especially the Indus) and extraction of water for irrigation has split the
populations and curbed their movements. Many hundreds are killed each year
by fishermen, often accidentally by drowning in fish-nets. They breed
throughout the year. Their population, estimated at 700 to one thousand, is
thought to be declining fast.

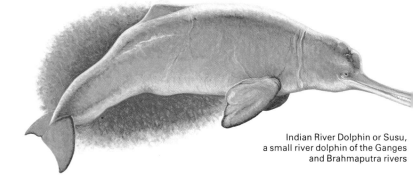

Indian River Dolphin or Susu,
a small river dolphin of the Ganges
and Brahmaputra rivers

Amazon River Dolphin or Boutu, a rare river dolphin of the Amazon and neighbouring rivers

Amazon River Dolphin (Boutu) *Inia geoffrensis* (Blainville 1818)

SIZE Nose-to-tail length 2–3 m. Sexes similar.

APPEARANCE Black or dark grey dorsally, pinkish-white flanks and abdomen; the young are generally darker than the adults. Bristles on the elongate snout; small eyes, barely visible between the chubby cheeks and bulbous forehead. The dorsal ridge rises to a long, flat dorsal fin. The flippers are pointed and the head twists and turns on a flexible neck. There are 25–30 sharp pointed teeth in each half-jaw.

RANGE Restricted to the Amazon, Negro and Maranon Rivers and their tributaries as far west as the Peruvian foothills of the Andes, and the Orinoco and Guaviare Rivers of Venezuela and Colombia.

A medium-sized river dolphin of northern South America, little studied in the field but tractable and friendly in captivity. The eyes are small but apparently functional; Boutus are reported to swim upside down, peering short-sightedly at the bottom in search of food, and also to rear frequently out of the water to see what is about. The snout is bristly, possibly as an aid to hunting in murky waters. Still plentiful, though widely dispersed over its extensive range; the total population is estimated at several thousand.

81

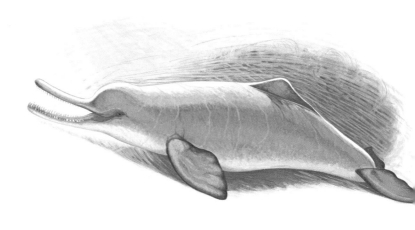

White Fin, Chinese Lake or White Flag Dolphin, found in a restricted area of the Yangzijiang

White Fin Dolphin (Beiji or Baijitun)   *Lipotes vexillifer*   (Miller 1918)

SIZE   Nose-to-tail length 1.5–2.5 m. Sexes similar. A specimen 1.5 m long weighed 60 kg.

APPEARANCE   Silver-grey above, paler grey below, with a long, slightly upturned snout and domed forehead. The dorsal fin rises high from the dorsal ridge, well toward the tail. Teeth small and sharp; over 30 in each half-jaw.

RANGE   Restricted to the mainstream of the lower and middle reaches of the Yangzijiang (Yangtse Kiang) River below Three Gorges, central China; also in neighbouring tributaries and the outlet of Dongting Hu (Lake Tung Ting).

A medium-sized river dolphin of which little is known except to local folk, and now to scientists of the Wuhan Institute of Hydrobiology who are studying it. Rare and rather timid, they live in muddy-bottomed rivers and lakes, hunting and travelling in small groups; their main foods are fish and crustaceans, which they stir from the bottom and probably hunt by sound rather than sight. White Fin Dolphins congregate in the river near Hongu in late spring and early summer when nursing their young. Though not heavily hunted, a few are caught each year on fishermen's lines and are valued for the medicinal qualities of their meat and fat. Some concern is felt for their future, and local scientists are seeing how they can best be protected.

La Plata or Franciscana River Dolphin, a dolphin of southern South American rivers and lakes

La Plata River Dolphin (Franciscana) *Pontoporia blainvillei* (Gervais and d'Orbigny 1844)

SIZE   Nose-to-tail length 1.5–2 m; females slightly larger than males.

APPEARANCE   A small tan or grey-brown dolphin, darker above and lighter below, with long flexible neck, prominent recurved dorsal fin and big flippers. Long, slender beak; teeth needle-like and very numerous – about 50 in each half-jaw.

RANGE   Numerous in La Plata estuary, less often seen in inshore waters of Argentina, Uruguay and Brazil between 42° and 32°S.

A shiny mud-coloured species; small groups are often seen swimming and diving around stationary ships in the muddy La Plata estuary, and many are caught in the nets of shark fishermen off Uruguay, where their biology has been studied. Their main food is fish, with squid, octopus and crustacea providing variety; much of their food seems to come from close to the sea bed. Calves measuring almost half the length of their mothers are born in spring, between September and January. The total population probably numbers tens of thousands, and is not thought to be endangered at present.

SUPERFAMILY ZIPHIOIDEA

FAMILY ZIPHIIDAE

This family includes five similar genera of medium-sized whales 5–10 m long. Slender, with small rounded or bulbous heads and tapering bottle-neck snouts, they occur in all the world's oceans. All ziphiids have one distinguishing mark – a pair of longitudinal grooves on the throat. All but one species have much-reduced teeth, possibly as an adaptation for catching and holding squid – their main food. Males have one or two pairs of teeth in the lower jaw and none in the upper, and females are toothless for most or all of their lives. Vestigial teeth are sometimes recorded. Tasman Beaked Whales alone have a full set of teeth in both jaws. The flippers are small; there is usually a big, recurving dorsal fin set well back towards the tail, and the tail flukes form a single crescent without a central notch.

FAMILY ZIPHIIDAE

Subfamily Ziphiinae

Tasmacetus shepherdi	Tasman Beaked Whale
Mesoplodon bidens	Sowerby's Beaked Whale
Mesoplodon europaeus	Gulf Stream Beaked Whale
Mesoplodon mirus	True's Beaked Whale
Mesoplodon pacificus	Longman's Beaked Whale
Mesoplodon grayi	Scamperdown Beaked Whale
Mesoplodon hectori	Hector's Beaked Whale
Mesoplodon stejnegeri	Stejneger's Beaked Whale
Mesoplodon carlhubbsi	Hubbs' Beaked Whale
Mesoplodon bowdoini	Andrews' Beaked Whale
Mesoplodon ginkgodens	Japanese Beaked Whale
Mesoplodon layardii	Strap-toothed Beaked Whale
Mesoplodon densirostris	de Blainville's Beaked Whale
Ziphius cavirostris	Goose-beaked Whale
Berardius bairdii	Northern Beaked Whale
Berardius arnuxii	Southern Beaked Whale
Hyperoodon ampullatus	Northern Bottlenose Whale
Hyperoodon planifrons	Southern Bottlenose Whale

Tasman Beaked Whale   *Tasmacetus shepherdi*   (Oliver 1937)

SIZE   Nose-to-tail length: males 8–9 m, females to 6.6 m, possibly longer.
APPEARANCE   Back and flanks dark, possibly striped, with pale tan or white underparts. The lower jaw is slightly longer than the upper; the beak as a whole is narrow, merging into a sloping forehead. There are 19 small flask-shaped teeth in each half of the upper jaw, and 26 in the lower, the leading pair larger and forming a double spike in males.

Tasman Beaked Whale

RANGE   So far restricted to the southern hemisphere; beached specimens have been found in New Zealand's South Island, Chubut, Argentina, and on Isla Mas Afuera, Juan Fernandez Archipelago, and a single live specimen may have been seen off New Zealand.

This mysterious small whale first appeared in New Zealand in 1937, and up to thirty-five years later only four specimens – all from the same region – had been identified. Two further specimens have now appeared off eastern and western South America, so the Tasman Beaked Whale – the only species of its family with full rows of teeth – appears to be a whale of southern temperate waters. Crabs, fish and squid beaks were found in the stomach of the Argentinian specimen. Virtually nothing else is known of the species' biology.

GENUS *Mesoplodon*

This is a group of dark blue-grey to black whales, very similar to each other in many respects and often hard to tell apart. All grow to lengths of 5–7 m; males may average slightly larger and heavier than females. The head is small, with a prominent bulging forehead and narrow beak; the lower jaw is narrow and slightly longer than the upper, and the throat grooves – probably there to allow stretching when bulky food is swallowed – lie very close to each other. The flippers are small and rounded; the dorsal fin is small and lies at least two thirds of the way along the body. A dozen species have been distinguished, mostly from a few beached specimens; in many of these the teeth of males (confined almost entirely to the lower jaw) are diagnostic; the teeth of females are smaller and may not appear through the gums. The hard horny gums in either sex are clearly adequate for catching and chopping the prey – believed to be mainly squid, and caught in deep water. Males often bear long double scratches on their flanks, suggesting that the paired teeth are used in sexual fighting. *Mesoplodon* whales seem to live in small, widely scattered groups far out at sea. Few whalers bother to hunt them, and they are not currently at risk from man.

As more specimens of this confusing genus appear, the pattern of their distribution is slowly clarifying. *M. bidens* and *stejnegeri* are northern cool-temperate species, respectively of the Atlantic and Pacific Oceans; *M. europaeus* lives in warmer north Atlantic waters, with *M. ginkgodens* and *carlhubbsi* its counterparts in the warmer Pacific Ocean. *M. pacificus* is a warm-water species of the southern Indian and Pacific Oceans; *M. hectori, grayi, mirus* and *bowdoini* are temperate southern species, which may also appear in northern oceans, and *M. layardii* may be similar, but has not yet appeared in the north. How these closely related species apportion the oceans' resources between them is an intriguing mystery that should keep cetologists guessing for many years.

Sowerby's Beaked Whale   *Mesoplodon bidens*   (Sowerby 1804)

Males have a single triangular tooth 8–9 cm tall about one third of the way along the lower jaw. This is a fairly common small whale of cool north Atlantic Ocean waters, generally far offshore. Many have been recorded in the North Sea and around the British Isles, fewer in the Baltic Sea, the Bay of Biscay and off New England and Newfoundland.

Gulf Stream Beaked Whale   *Mesoplodon europaeus*   (Gervais 1855)

A rather rare species, similar to the Sowerby's Beaked Whale but usually found in warmer Atlantic waters; though first described from an English Channel specimen, this species is more often found off Florida and in the Caribbean. Males have one very small triangular tooth, barely visible, about half of the way along either side of the lower jaw. A 4.5-metre-long cow with a 2.25-metre-long calf, apparently new-born, was recorded in Jamaica in February.

True's Beaked Whale   *Mesoplodon mirus*   (True 1913)

Males have one pair of small, flat triangular teeth visible in the tips of the lower jaw; females too have them, but hidden by the gums. A species fairly often found stranded in New England, more rarely in western Britain, it was until recently thought to be confined to the north Atlantic. However, very similar animals with distinctive pale patches on throat and flippers (including a lactating cow and calf) have also been washed up off southern Africa, suggesting that there are breeding stocks in both northern and southern temperate waters.

Longman's Beaked Whale   *Mesoplodon pacificus*   (Longman 1926)

Even rarer than most other species of the genus, Longman's Beaked Whale is known from two skulls found on Australian beaches thirty years apart, and a third one found more recently in Somalia. It has not yet been described in the flesh, and its biology is unknown. Some authorities refer it to a separate genus *Indopacetus*; we shall be in a better position to decide when we know more of it than its skull.

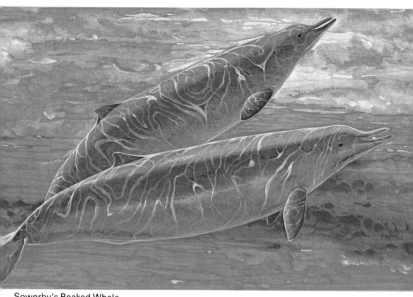

Sowerby's Beaked Whale

Gulf Stream Beaked Whale

True's Beaked Whale

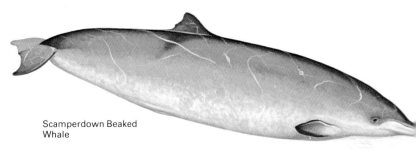
Scamperdown Beaked
Whale

Scamperdown Beaked Whale   *Mesoplodon grayi*   (von Haast 1876)

A very dark grey species with pale upper lip, chin, throat and flanks and dark longitudinal midventral band: some specimens are black all over. Males have a small triangular tooth on either side at the point where the two mandibles split; tiny teeth are sometimes found in the rear half of the upper jaw as well. First recorded from New Zealand waters, later from Patagonia, Australia and South Africa, it is mainly a species of the southern temperate zone. However, a specimen was stranded on the Netherlands coast in 1927.

Andrews' Beaked Whale   *Mesoplodon bowdoini*   (Andrews 1908)

This species, a slightly smaller southern counterpart of Stejneger's and Hubbs' Beaked Whales, was described originally from a specimen stranded on a New Zealand beach. A few further specimens have since appeared in the New Zealand area, but the species has only doubtfully been recorded elsewhere. The single teeth, set much as in Stejneger's Whale, are broad-based and flat, but lean outward and taper to a point.

Hubbs' Beaked Whale   *Mesoplodon carlhubbsi*   (Moore 1963)

A species similar to Stejneger's Beaked Whale, with a single large, slightly curving rectangular tooth, 9 cm long and 16–17 cm high, on either side of the lower jaw. There are minor differences in the shape of the skull. This species has so far been found only in temperate waters of the north Pacific Ocean – beached in California and Washington, and caught commercially in deep water off central Japan.

Stejneger's Beaked Whale   *Mesoplodon stejnegeri*   (True 1885)

A uniformly black species of the northern Pacific Ocean, found mainly in sub-Arctic waters but ranging from Japan to the Commander and Pribilof Islands, Alaska and British Columbia. Males have one large, flat, slab-sided rectangular tooth 8–14 cm long, one third to half-way along the lower jaw on either side; these show prominently in the living animal. They are reported to gather in small groups on the salmon grounds off the western United States.

88

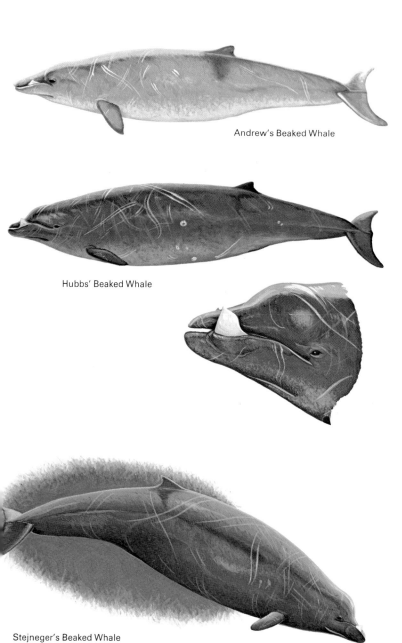

Andrew's Beaked Whale

Hubbs' Beaked Whale

Stejneger's Beaked Whale

Strap-toothed Whale

Hector's Beaked Whale *Mesoplodon hectori* (Gray 1871)

Previously known only from the southern hemisphere, this species has now appeared off California as well. There have been several strandings in New Zealand and Tasmanian waters, and immature specimens have been washed up on beaches in the Falkland Islands, Tierra del Fuego and South Africa. Californian specimens have included adults of both sexes, an immature male and a calf. Males carry two large, triangular teeth close to the tip of the lower jaw. There are no clear illustrations of this species; they seem to be dark grey animals with white under the tail flukes, possibly a pale chin, and a short beak.

Strap-toothed Beaked Whale *Mesoplodon layardii* (Gray 1865)

This is a little-known but widespread species of southern temperate waters. Probably the largest of the genus, many have been stranded in New Zealand, fewer in Australia, South Africa, Chile and the Falkland Islands. Charcoal grey or black dorsally, paler on the flanks and abdomen, they gain their name from the teeth of the males; one on either side grows upward and back from the mid-point of the lower jaw, curving outward to wrap around the rostrum (beak), apparently restricting the mouth. A female stranded in New Zealand in September had recently calved.

Japanese Beaked Whale *Mesoplodon ginkgodens* (Nishiwaki and Kamiya 1958)

Relatively recently described from beached specimens in Japanese waters, these whales are entirely black above and beneath. Up to 4.7 m long, they have a single flat tooth half-way along the lower jaw, shaped like the leaf of a ginkgo tree; the teeth do not erupt in cows, and in bulls are all but hidden by the deep lower lip. Several have now been recovered from Japan and Taiwan, though it seems to be a rare species.

de Blainville's Beaked Whale *Mesoplodon densirostris* (Blainville 1817)

A widely distributed, rare species, recorded from the Seychelle Islands, Madeira, Spain, Hawaii, the southern Pacific and the eastern coast of North America. Black or dark grey, with an unusually large dorsal fin, this species has a deep lower jaw with a single large, flat tooth set in a bony crest midway along either side.

90

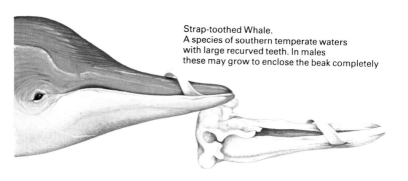

Strap-toothed Whale.
A species of southern temperate waters
with large recurved teeth. In males
these may grow to enclose the beak completely

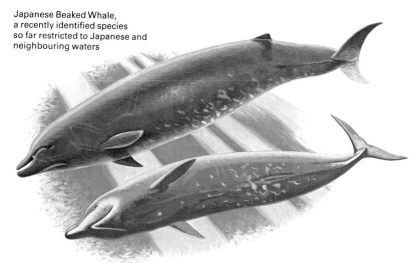

Japanese Beaked Whale,
a recently identified species
so far restricted to Japanese and
neighbouring waters

de Blainville's Beaked Whale,
widely distributed
in tropical and subtropical
waters on either side
of the equator

Goose-beaked Whale. A pale-headed species of wide distribution; the body may be grey, blue-black or brown

Goose-beaked Whale   *Ziphius cavirostris*   (G. Cuvier 1823)

SIZE   Nose-to-tail length: males up to 6.7 m, females slightly longer. Large specimens weigh 5 tonnes or more.
APPEARANCE   A medium-sized whale with short beak; grey or black with white chin, face and throat, and varying patterns of white spots, flecks and scratches. In either sex there are two small cylindrical teeth, sharply spiked, set in the jutting point of the lower jaw; these are visible only in males.
RANGE   Completely cosmopolitan in temperate and tropical waters, from Sweden and Alaska in the north to Cape Horn, South Africa and New Zealand in the south, including the Mediterranean Sea.

Known mostly from specimens stranded in Britain and the United States, this species is also hunted commercially on a small scale in Japan. A whale of deep offshore waters, it feeds on squid and fish; at sea single animals or schools of two to seven are generally reported. Though widespread it is by no means common, and little is known of its biology.

Northern Beaked Whale   *Berardius bairdii*   (Stejneger 1883)

SIZE   Nose-to-tail 10–12 m or longer; weight of large specimens 12 tonnes and more.
APPEARANCE   Silvery to dark grey dorsally, paler ventrally; a slender whale with prominent forehead and well-defined beak. Males show two pairs of flat, triangular teeth on either side of the lip of the lower jaw.
RANGE   Restricted to the colder waters of the northern Pacific Ocean, from the Bering Sea and Sea of Okhotsk to Alaska; occasionally found as far south as south-eastern Japan and southern California.

This species, the northern counterpart of *B. arnuxii* and largest of all the beaked whales, wanders the northern Pacific Ocean. It is known mostly from beached specimens, but local small-scale hunting off Canada, the US and Japan has yielded further information. Usually found well offshore, it feeds in deep water on squid, fish and bottom-living invertebrates. Calves are 4–5 m long at birth, and females probably breed every third year. Though stocks may have declined off Japan, where fishing has been heaviest, the species as a whole is probably not at risk from man.

Southern Beaked Whale. This and the Northern Beaked Whale (*below*) have two teeth on either side of the lower jaw tip

Southern Beaked Whale *Berardius arnuxii* (Duvernoy 1851)

SIZE   Nose-to-tail length about 10 m; weight 8 tonnes.

APPEARANCE   A medium-sized dark grey whale, paler on flanks and abdomen. Beak and forehead are prominent. Males have two flat triangular teeth on either side of the lower jaw, the front pair 7–8 cm long, the rear ones slightly smaller.

RANGE   A species of southern cool and cold waters; there have been several strandings in New Zealand and others in southern Australia, South Africa, southern South America, the Falkland Islands, South Georgia and in the Antarctic Peninsula area.

This little-known whale travels singly or in small groups of three or four. A deep-sea species, it probably feeds on squid and fish, though little is known of its ecology.

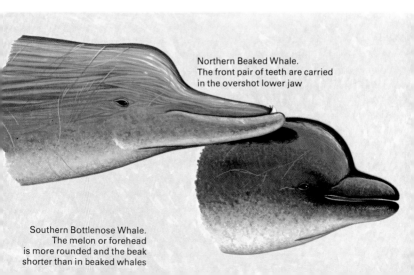

Northern Beaked Whale. The front pair of teeth are carried in the overshot lower jaw

Southern Bottlenose Whale. The melon or forehead is more rounded and the beak shorter than in beaked whales

Northern (blue) and Southern (grey) Bottlenose whales;
colour in both species varies from grey-black to pale blue-grey

Northern Bottlenose Whale   *Hyperoodon ampullatus*   (Forster 1770)

SIZE   Nose-to-tail length: males to 9.5 m, females 7–8 m. A female 7 m long weighed almost 3 tonnes.

APPEARANCE   A fat, well-padded, medium-sized whale, blue-grey, dark brown or black on top, paler on chest and abdomen; bulbous forehead, short but well-defined 'bottleneck' rostrum. Large, recurved dorsal fin set well back along the body. Two small cylindrical or oval-section teeth at the tip of the lower jaw, visible only in males.

RANGE   A species of cool north Atlantic waters, ranging north to the ice edge – well into the Arctic basin – in summer, and south to Florida, the Cape Verde Islands and beyond in winter. Usually found offshore; beached specimens have been recorded from both sides of the Atlantic. Rather doubtfully recorded also in the north Pacific Ocean.

Hunting for over a century by Canadians and Norwegians has made this by far the best-known member of its family. There are probably several discrete stocks that move northward into Arctic waters in spring to feed below the rich summer plankton, and head southward again in autumn. Most hunting takes place in summer, when the whales are fattening. Most strandings occur in late summer and autumn, especially during the southward movement. Northern

Bottlenose Whales feed mainly on deep-water squid, but also take bottom-living invertebrates (sea stars, sea cucumbers, etc.) and pelagic herrings. Cows give birth in April, probably every second year. Three metres long at birth, the calves stay by their mothers for at least a year. Lifespan probably exceeds thirty-five years. Despite intermittent hunting the stocks of this species are not seriously endangered at present.

Southern Bottlenose Whale   *Hyperoodon planifrons*   (Flower 1882)

SIZE   Nose-to-tail length 6–7.5 m: weight 3–4 tonnes.
APPEARANCE   Similar in most respects to the Northern Bottlenose Whale.
RANGE   A widely ranging species of southern cool waters; found off the coasts of New Zealand, South Africa and South America, and also in Antarctic waters in summer.

Known only from a few stranded specimens and sightings at sea, this is a widespread but rarely reported species. A few have been taken by southern whalers, but the stocks are too small and widely scattered to be hunted commercially.

SUPERFAMILY PHYSETEROIDEA

FAMILY PHYSETERIDAE

This small but distinctive family includes only three species, different enough to merit two separate subfamilies – the Physeterinae (Sperm Whales only) and the Kogiinae (Pygmy and Dwarf Sperm Whales). Characters uniting the family include the large spermaceti organ in the head (a reservoir of waxy oil, providing both buoyancy and foam-producing oil for nitrogen absorption, see p. 96); an enlarged left nostril, giving a distinctive spout, and a small mouth with narrow lower jaw; there are further anatomical points not visible from outside. The two subfamilies differ markedly in size and proportions. Sperm Whales are the largest of the Odontoceti, with enormous heads and body proportions similar to those of the large mysticetes. Pygmy and Dwarf Sperm Whales are among the smallest odontocetes, with tiny heads and dolphin-like proportions.

FAMILY PHYSETERIDAE

Subfamily Physeterinae
  Physeter catodon   Sperm Whale
Subfamily Kogiinae
  Kogia breviceps   Pygmy Sperm Whale
  Kogia simus   Dwarf Sperm Whale

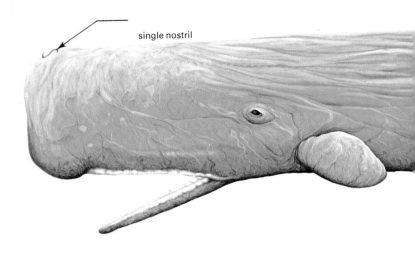

single nostril

Sperm Whale *Physeter catodon* Linnaeus 1758

SIZE Nose-to-tail length: males 15–18 m, weighing up to 55 tonnes; females 10–12 m, weighing up to 16 tonnes.
APPEARANCE Large grey or brown slab-sided whales; the huge rectangular head with its relatively tiny mouth seems to occupy about one third of the total body length. Blunt dorsal ridge with graded serrations; no dorsal fin. Small flippers; tail flukes rounded with central notch. There are 18–25 large spike teeth on either side of the lower jaw; vestigial teeth only in upper jaw.
RANGE Widely distributed in all oceans. Cows and calves are found especially in warm latitudes; bulls migrate annually into colder water.

An unmistakable species – the single nostril on the left side of the head spouts forward and outward. Largest of all the odontocetes, this is probably also the deepest diver (reaching over 1000 m) with the longest staying-down time (over an hour). It feeds on squid and fish, including sharks; the face is often scarred by sucker-marks of giant squid, caught and eaten at great depths. Cows produce their young every third or fourth year, moving into warm seas to give birth. The calves may measure 4 m or more at birth, and are weaned in cooler waters where feeding is better. Sperm Whale cows, calves and juveniles form social groups of ten to twenty which may aggregate into bigger herds; these are joined by single large bulls in the mating season. Young bulls form separate bachelor herds. Bulls wander further into cold seas than cows, so more of them are taken by whalers in high latitudes. Sperm Whales have been hunted commercially for centuries; tens of thousands have been taken annually during recent years by the pelagic whaling fleets. Their oil, with different qualities from that of other whales, has been valued especially as a fuel, fine lubricant, leather dressing and basis for cosmetics. Some stocks now show serious indications of decline, and the number killed each year is falling steadily. With pressure of public opinion mounting against whaling and whale products, there is currently every indication that Sperm Whales will outlast the industry which has for so long persecuted them.

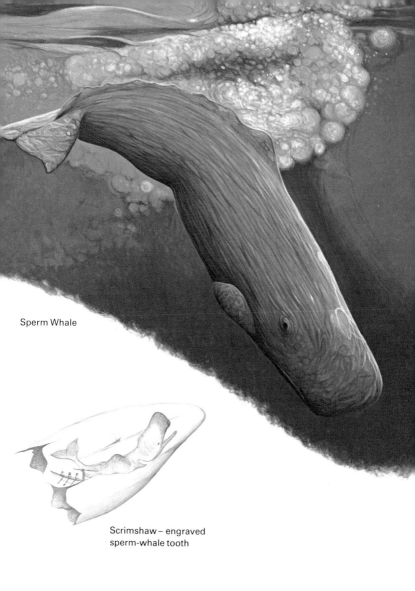

Sperm Whale

Scrimshaw – engraved
sperm-whale tooth

Pygmy Sperm Whale

Dwarf Sperm Whale

Pygmy Sperm Whale   *Kogia breviceps*   (Blainville 1838)

SIZE   Nose-to-tail length 2.7–3.4 m, weight 300–400 kg.
APPEARANCE   Small, dolphin-like whales with short rounded head and narrow lower jaw; grey, black or dark brown above, paler below. There are 12–16 fine curved teeth on either side of the lower jaw, sharp but lacking enamel. The dorsal fin is low, set well back along the body.
RANGE   Tropical and warm temperate waters of all oceans; most strandings have occurred in the southern United States, southern Africa, south-eastern Australia and New Zealand.

A rather rare and timid species, widely distributed in warm oceans but nowhere plentiful; often found in small groups of three or four. Little is known of its biology. Pygmy Sperm Whales are hunted spasmodically and on a local scale in the Pacific Ocean, but with little effect on their total stocks. They feed mainly on squid and fish, and are assumed to be deep divers.

Dwarf Sperm Whale   *Kogia simus*   (Owen 1866)

SIZE   Nose-to-tail length: 2.0–2.7 m; weight 130–270 kg.
APPEARANCE   Small, rather shapeless whales, lacking the fine lines of most dolphins and porpoises; grey, black or dark brown dorsally, paler ventrally. The teeth, 8–12 on either side of the lower jaw, are thin, like curved needles, and lack enamel. There is a large dorsal fin near the mid-point of the back.
RANGE   Found sparsely in all tropical and warm temperate waters, generally in warmer latitudes than Pygmy Sperm Whales. Most strandings have been recorded off Japan and the eastern United States; others have occurred as far apart as southern Africa, India, southern Australia and Hawaii.

This species has for long been confused with its congener the Pygmy Sperm Whale; however it is much smaller and more slender at all stages of growth. Little is known of the biology of Dwarf Sperm Whales. They appear to spend most of their lives over deep waters, living in small groups of three to six and feeding mainly on squid and fish.

SUPERFAMILY MONODONTOIDEA

FAMILY MONODONTIDAE

This tiny family contains only two species in separate genera. These are primitive whales, lacking some of the sophisticated structures (for example of the ear sinuses) that give more advanced whales their greater efficiency. Both species are restricted to Arctic waters, where lack of competition from other whales may have helped them to survive.

FAMILY MONODONTIDAE

Subfamily Monodontinae
Monodon monoceros — Narwhal
Delphinapteras leucas — Beluga (White Whale)

Narwhal   *Monodon monoceros*   Linnaeus 1758

SIZE   Nose-to-tail length: males 4–5 m (excluding the tusk); weight 1.2–1.6 tonnes. Females slightly smaller.

APPEARANCE   Silver-grey mottles, paling with age; dark brown-grey on the face, back, flippers and tail, paler on the flanks and abdomen. Males carry a spirally twisted tusk, a vastly overgrown canine tooth which may grow to 2 m or more. Tusks are occasionally paired, rarely found in females; there are no other functional teeth.

RANGE   Formerly widespread in the Arctic, now rare in accessible parts of the European, Asian and Alaskan sectors, though still quite plentiful in the Canadian Arctic; found even in the pack-ice close to the Pole. Wanderers range south to Britain and northern Europe.

Narwhal

A fat, chubby whale with short flippers and little or no dorsal fin, still fairly common in Canadian and Greenland waters where a population of at least 10,000 is estimated. Elsewhere it has been driven from shallow seas by local hunting. Docile and readily caught by netting or harpooning, it has for long provided meat and oil for northern man; the skin, regarded as a special delicacy, has recently been shown to contain significant amounts of vitamin C. Several hundred are still taken annually at the ice edge by Canadian and Greenland Eskimos. The tusks, used by the males in sexual display and fighting, are said to have inspired the legend of the unicorn. Narwhals feed on squid, fish and crustaceans, caught mainly in deep water. Their single (rarely paired) calves are born in late summer, 1.6 m long and weighing 80 kg. Cows probably breed every three years.

Beluga (White Whale) *Delphinapterus leucas* (Pallas 1776)

SIZE   Nose-to-tail length 4–5 m; females slightly smaller than males; the largest males probably weigh up to 1.6 tonnes.
APPEARANCE   Adults are pearly-white, younger animals grey or mottled. There is a distinct neck; the head is bulbous, with a short beak, and there is no dorsal fin. Teeth: 8–11 pairs, blunt and peg-like, in either jaw.
RANGE   An Arctic and sub-Arctic species, mainly coastal and estuarine; there are about seven discrete stocks living in the Gulf of St Lawrence, Hudson Bay, Cumberland Sound, the White, Barents, Kara, Beaufort, Bering and Okhotsk Seas, and off Kamchatka and Alaska. Vagrants have been stranded in Britain and New England, well south of their usual range.

This ghostly white whale lives in groups of ten to twenty, forming herds of several hundred during their annual migrations. They are fish-eaters, noted for their trilling, canary-like calls used in hunting. Belugas gather to mate in spring, and feed in wandering herds through the summer, shifting their hunting grounds with the movements of the pack-ice. Gestation takes fifteen months, and the herds congregate in the warm water of estuaries to calve in July and August. The calves, 1.5–2 m long at birth, remain with their mothers for over a year. Belugas have long been hunted for their meat and oil, both by natives and by commercial whalers who drove them ashore in bays. A few hundred are still taken by native hunters every year, and interference from boats, river barrages, oil rigs and pollution may be taking an additional toll. The North American population is estimated at 30,000.

Beluga

SUPERFAMILY DELPHINOIDEA

This superfamily links three families of mostly small cetaceans – the real dolphins and porpoises. They are the Stenidae (long-beaked dolphins), the Phocidae (porpoises) and the Delphinidae (ocean dolphins), together mustering thirty-seven species in fourteen genera. Nearly all are within the 1.5–3 m range, but a few – for example the Killer Whales and Pilot Whales – are far bigger and truly whale-sized. All the delphinoids are slender, fast-moving creatures, elegantly patterned with stripes, spots and criss-crossed lines superimposed on basic counter-shading (dark above, light below). These are the cetaceans most likely to be found riding the bow-wave of a ship, playing happily with children in shallow water, nosing around divers to see what they are doing, and jumping through hoops in circus acts. Their characteristic 'porpoising' – leaping through the air while swimming at speed – means more than high spirits; it is a way of saving energy. Sharp-witted, intelligent, and superbly equipped for their way of life, delphinoids show many advances in anatomy and behaviour over the rest of the toothed whales.

FAMILY STENIDAE

This small family of warm-water dolphins includes four species, all little-known and included in the three genera *Steno*, *Sousa* and *Sotalia*. Family characters include a long beak merging smoothly into the forehead and a recurved dorsal fin.

FAMILY STENIDAE

Steno bredanensis	Rough-toothed Dolphin
Sotalia fluviatilis	Tucuxi
Sousa chinensis	Indo-Pacific Humpback Dolphin
Sousa teuszii	Atlantic Humpback Dolphin

Rough-toothed Dolphin   *Steno bredanensis*   (Lesson 1828)

SIZE   Nose-to-tail length 2.2–2.7 m.
APPEARANCE   A grey, well-streamlined dolphin, with dark back and paler, spotted flanks and belly. The snout is long, the flippers are narrow and elegantly pointed, and the dorsal fin stands tall. There are about 24 pairs of *ridged* teeth in either jaw – hence the popular name.
RANGE   Found sparsely in tropical and subtropical waters world-wide, including the Mediterranean Sea. A deep-water species, seldom found inshore.

Very little information is available on this species, though many strandings have been reported throughout its wide range, and several have been kept in captivity. Rough-toothed Dolphins are occasionally taken by commercial fishermen or caught accidentally in tuna nets, but the species normally lives too far from land to be troubled by inshore whalers, and is too small and widely dispersed to be hunted – or even studied – systematically.

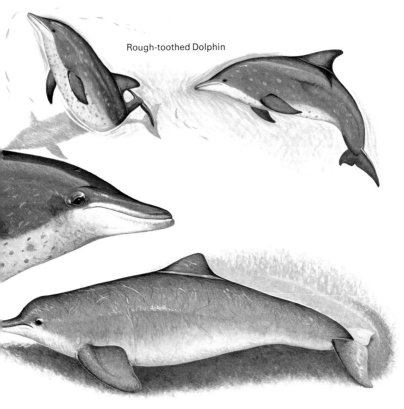

Rough-toothed Dolphin

Tucuxi

Tucuxi *Sotalia fluviatilis* (Gervais 1853)

SIZE   Nose-to-tail length 1.5–2.0 m; mature individuals can be little over 1 m long.
Weight to about 50 kg.
APPEARANCE   A tiny grey-brown dolphin with yellow or white flanks and abdomen;
often seen in small groups in bays, coastal waters and estuaries of South America.
Teeth: 30–32, sharply pointed, in each half of both jaws.
RANGE   Restricted to warm South American east-coastal waters and rivers, ranging
from Santos and Rio de Janeiro in the south to Venezuela (including Lake Maracaibo) in
the north; plentiful also in the Amazon and its tributaries, and the Orinoco River, where
it lives in association with its up-country cousins, the Boutus or Amazon River Dolphins.

Though well-known and quite plentiful in South American ports and rivers,
this dolphin has received very little study. In the past, five or more separate
species have been postulated. It is possible, even likely, that there are local
variations in size, proportions and colour between the different stocks, which
may well be geographically isolated from each other. But current wisdom
places them all in a single species under the name of the first one described.

Indo-Pacific Humpback Dolphin

Indo-Pacific Humpback Dolphin *Sousa chinensis* (Osbeck 1765)

SIZE   Nose-to-tail length 1.5–3 m; weight to about 300 kg.

APPEARANCE   A chunky dolphin with thickened dorsal ridge supporting a long dorsal fin and extending well into the tail. Colour of adults varies geographically from pure white or cream (Australasia, Indonesia, China) to leaden grey speckled with brown (India) and grey with darker grey stripes and flecks, and a tendency to pale with age (East Africa). There are 30–50 sharply pointed teeth in each half of both jaws.

RANGE   A widely ranging species, mainly of coastal waters, found off South and East Africa, in the Red Sea and Persian Gulf, off India, Indonesia, New Guinea, northern Australia and southern China.

Another little-known dolphin. Marked geographical colour variation has caused it to be described under at least four separate species names; the conservative approach is to list all under the first name and leave others to justify the remaining ones when more rigorous studies have been completed. Said to be a fish-eater, it has been kept successfully in captivity. A new-born calf, off-white, just over 1 m long and weighing 15.5 kg, was recorded off South Africa. Young of this stock become progressively more grey as they approach maturity; adults increase in girth, developing a white dorsal fin and hump and white tips to the nose and tail flukes. Many bear scars on their dorsal fin and tail, including severe shark bites.

Atlantic Humpback Dolphin

Atlantic Humpback Dolphin   *Sousa teuszii*   (Kuekenthal 1892)

SIZE   Nose-to-tail length 1.8–2.2 m. Weight about 100 kg.
APPEARANCE   A grey-brown dolphin with the distinctive raised dorsal ridge and long dorsal fin of its genus. There are 27–30 teeth in each half-jaw.
RANGE   Coastal waters of tropical West Africa, probably from Mauretania to Angola.

Least known of all the long-beaked dolphins, this species has been described from fewer than half a dozen complete specimens.

FAMILY PHOCOENIDAE

This family of six closely related species includes all the delphinoids that Britons call 'porpoise'. They are small, rather chubby whales with a rounded, beakless face, and about twenty-three pairs of flattened or spade-shaped teeth in either jaw. The dorsal fin, if present, is triangular – never recurved. Americans use 'porpoise' in a broader sense to cover some of the smaller Delphinidae as well.

FAMILY PHOCOENIDAE

Subfamily Phocoeninae
   Phocoena phocoena   Common (Harbour) Porpoise
   Phocoena sinus   Californian Porpoise (Cochito)
   Phocoena spinipinnis   Burmeister's Porpoise
   Phocoena dioptrica   Spectacled Porpoise
   Neophocoena phocaenoides   Black Finless Porpoise
   Phocoenoides dalli   Dall's Porpoise

Common Porpoises

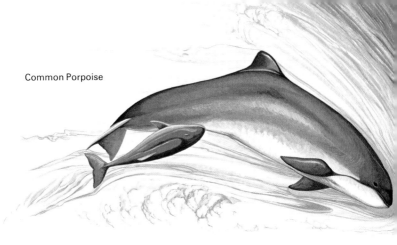

Common Porpoise

Common (Harbour) Porpoise   *Phocoena phocoena*   (Linnaeus 1758)

SIZE   Nose-to-tail length 1.5–1.8 m; weight to 90 kg. Females may average slightly larger than males.

APPEARANCE   Fat, cheerful little porpoises that dodge in and out of harbours and estuaries like oversized mice. Black or dark grey head, back, flippers and tail, white or pale grey flanks and underparts. About 23 pairs of sharp flattened teeth in either jaw.

RANGE   World-wide distribution in the northern hemisphere, from the Arctic fringes to the edge of the tropics, including the Mediterranean and Black Sea. Many stocks seem to be very limited in range, performing local migrations but remaining isolated.

One of the best-known of all porpoises from its prevalence in harbours, estuaries and bays, and its frequent stranding on beaches. Timid and fast-moving, Harbour Porpoises are not easy to handle and do not take readily to captivity. They reach maturity at three to four years, and cows probably calve every year thereafter. Calves at birth measure 0.75 m and weigh 5–6 kg. Harbour porpoises travel in small schools of five to twenty, occasionally aggregating into huge groups of several hundred. They feed mainly on fish, and many are caught and drowned accidentally each year in fishing nets. Many more – probably tens of thousands altogether – are killed each year by netting and driving on hunting grounds as far apart as Iceland, the Baltic and the Black Sea. Stocks are affected locally by hunting, but the species as a whole continues to flourish.

Californian Porpoise

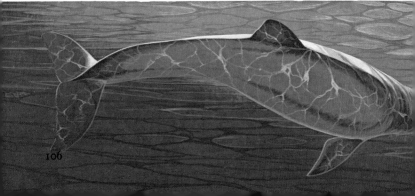

Californian Porpoise (Cochito) *Phocoena sinus* (Norris and McFarland 1958)

SIZE   Nose-to-tail length 1.4–1.5 m (small sample).
APPEARANCE   A very small dark blue-grey porpoise; 20–23 pairs of spade-shaped teeth in either jaw.
RANGE   Restricted to the Gulf of California, mostly to the northern end.

This small porpoise of very restricted range was only recently identified as a species in its own right, and little has so far been discovered about its biology. It feeds on fish, very often getting mixed up in the nets of inshore fishermen. Though nowhere hunted commercially, accidental losses are high for so small and limited a stock, and some concern is felt for its future.

Spectacled Porpoise   *Phocoena dioptrica*   (Lahille 1912)

SIZE   Nose-to-tail length 1.8–2.0 m; weight about 50 kg.
APPEARANCE   Black dorsally with white underparts and flanks. The eyes, set in the white part of the face, are ringed with black. There are 20–25 pairs of teeth in either jaw.
RANGE   East coast of South America from Uruguay southward to Tierra del Fuego; known also from the Falkland Islands and South Georgia.

A rare porpoise, which has apparently never been examined live; nothing is known of its biology.

Spectacled Porpoise

Black Finless Porpoise *Neophocoena phocaenoides* (Cuvier 1829)

SIZE   Nose-to-tail length 1.5 m: weight about 35 kg.
APPEARANCE   A small grey-black porpoise with a dorsal ridge but no dorsal fin. The flippers are large and pointed, the tail flukes deeply notched. Teeth: 15–25 in each half-jaw.
RANGE   A coastal, inshore and riverine species of southern and eastern Asia, occurring from the Persian Gulf to Pakistan, India, Malaya, Indonesia, China and Japan – often in association with mangroves. It occurs also in the Yangzijiang (Yangtse Kiang) River and Dongting Hu (Lake Tung Ting). There appear to be three major stocks – Indo-Malayan, Chinese and Japanese – which some authors regard as distinct races or even species.

These distinctive little porpoises live in sheltered coastal waters, rivers and salt-marshes, feeding on fish, octopuses and crustaceans. Very little is known of their biology.

Burmeister's Porpoise *Phocoena spinipinnis* (Burmeister 1865)

SIZE   Nose-to-tail length 1.9 m; weight about 50 kg.
APPEARANCE   An all-black porpoise with flat forehead and sharply cut-off dorsal fin. There are about 20 pairs of teeth in either jaw.
RANGE   Southern South America – on the east coast as far north as Uruguay, in the west almost to the Equator; common in the Falkland Islands.

A fairly well-known porpoise within its range, often caught by fishermen in nets set close inshore and sold as butchers' meat in Peru, Chile and Uruguay. Science knows very little of the species, which may be at risk from the local hunting.

Dall's Porpoise *Phocoenoides dalli* (True 1885)

SIZE   Nose-to-tail length: males 1.8–2.1 m; females probably slightly smaller. Weight 100–150 kg.
APPEARANCE   A fat, chunky black porpoise with a conspicuous white patch on the abdomen and sides; the tip and rear edge of the tail fin are also white. Teeth absent.
RANGE   A species of the temperate and cold northern Pacific Ocean, ranging from eastern Japan and the Sea of Okhotsk (where the local form has been called *P. truei*) to Baja California, and penetrating north into the southern Bering Sea. Mainly coastal, but found also in offshore waters.

A lively, fast-moving porpoise that tumbles through the water in groups of three to five, rarely more. Winter finds them close to the coasts; in summer they move northward and spend more time in deeper water. Most births occur in July and August; the new-born calves, about a metre long, are toned-down replicas of their parents. Dall's Porpoises feed mainly on surface-living fish, often falling foul of nets; about 10,000 per year are caught accidentally by Japanese fishermen alone, and several thousand more are harpooned each year for food.

Black Finless Porpoise

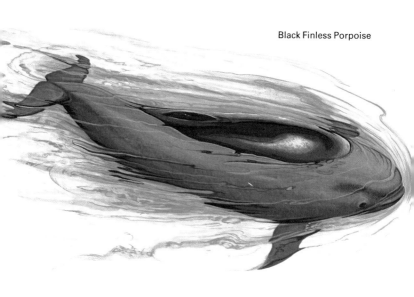

Burmeister's Porpoise

Dall's Porpoise

FAMILY DELPHINIDAE

Largest of the delphinoid families, this is a composite group of twenty-seven species divided for convenience into four subfamilies – the Orcinae (pilot whales, killer whales and their kin), Lissodelphinae (right whale dolphins), Cephalorhynchinae (Commerson's and other black and white dolphins), and Delphininae ('true' dolphins). Most of the family and subfamily characteristics are small points of internal anatomy; overall the delphinids are slender, sleek, with well-developed rostrum and cylindrical pointed teeth, and nearly all have a strong, recurved dorsal fin.

FAMILY DELPHINIDAE

Subfamily Orcinae
Globicephala malaena (two races) — Long-finned Pilot Whale
Globicephala macrorhynchus — Short-finned Pilot Whale
Orcaella brevirostris — Irrawaddy Dolphin
Feresa attenuata — Pygmy Killer Whale
Pseudorca crassidens — False Killer Whale
Orcinus orca — Killer Whale

Subfamily Lissodelphinae
Lissodelphis borealis — Northern Right Whale Dolphin
Lissodelphis peronii — Southern Right Whale Dolphin

Subfamily Cephalorhynchinae
Cephalorhynchus commersonii — Commerson's Dolphin
Cephalorhynchus eutropia — White-bellied (Chilean) Dolphin
Cephalorhynchus heavisidii — Heaviside's Dolphin
Cephalorhynchus hectori — Hector's Dolphin

Subfamily Delphininae
Delphinus delphis — Common Dolphin
Lagenorhynchus albirostris — White-beaked Dolphin
Lagenorhynchus acutus — Atlantic White-sided Dolphin
Lagenorhynchus obliquidens — Pacific White-sided Dolphin
Lagenorhynchus obscurus — Dusky Dolphin
Lagenorhynchus cruciger — Hourglass Dolphin
Lagenorhynchus australis — Peale's Dolphin
Peponocephala electra — Melon-headed Dolphin
Lagenodelphis hosei — Fraser's Dolphin
Stenella longirostris — Spinner Dolphin
Stenella coeruleoalba — Striped (Euphrosyne) Dolphin
Stenella attenuata — Pacific Spotted Dolphin
Stenella plagiodon — Atlantic Spotted Dolphin
Tursiops truncatus — Bottlenose Dolphin
Grampus griseus — Risso's Dolphin

Long-finned Pilot Whale

Long-finned Pilot Whale *Globicephala malaena* (Traill 1809)

SIZE   Nose-to-tail length: males 4.5–6 m; females 4–5 m.

APPEARANCE   A long, cylindrical black dolphin with a small grey patch behind each eye and a larger grey 'saddle' behind the dorsal fin – which is strongly hooked and well forward – starting almost over the long, slender flippers. Bulging forehead; 7–12 strong teeth in each half-jaw.

RANGE   There are two geographically separated races (some authorities list them as full species) occupying the southern and northern cool temperate zones: (i) *G.m. malaena* of the north Atlantic Ocean, from New England in the west to Greenland, Iceland, Scandinavia, the Baltic (rarely), the North Sea, Britain, France and the Mediterranean; (ii) *G.m. edwardi* of the southern Atlantic, Indian, Pacific and Southern Oceans.

Large, highly sociable dolphins often seen going about their business in groups of several hundred. They feed on fish – both bottom-living and pelagic – and squid, probably diving deep when necessary. Cows start to breed at six years, producing a calf every third year. Gestation takes sixteen months and the calves – well over a metre long at birth – are fed on milk for over eighteen months. Big schools of Pilot Whales close inshore easily become stranded, and can readily be driven ashore by hunters; many thousands have been taken in Newfoundland, the Faroe Islands and other centres. Stocks have probably been depleted locally, but the species as a whole is not endangered.

Short-finned Pilot Whale

Short-finned Pilot Whale   *Globicephala macrorhynchus*   (Gray 1846)

SIZE   Nose-to-tail length: males 4.8–5.3 m; females 3.2–4.0 m.
APPEARANCE   A large, slender black dolphin with cylindrical body and strongly hooked dorsal fin. There are 7–12 pairs of teeth in either jaw.
RANGE   Tropical and warm temperate waters of the Atlantic, Indian and Pacific Oceans. There may be several distinctive stocks or races.

A species difficult to distinguish from its long-finned cousin, though generally found in warmer waters of both hemispheres; very similar in appearance, biology and way of life. Widely hunted by driving in the Caribbean, on tropical mid-oceanic islands and in Japan, its stocks suffer local depletion, but the species as a whole appears to be plentiful.

Irrawaddy Dolphin   *Orcaella brevirostris*   (Gray 1866)

SIZE   Nose-to-tail length about 2 m; weight 80–100 kg.
APPEARANCE   A grey dolphin, dark or pale, with round head, short rostrum and flexible neck. Large paddle-shaped flippers; squat, recurved dorsal fin set well back along the body. Teeth: between 10 and 20 pairs in either jaw.
RANGE   Restricted to tropical waters of the Indian and Pacific Oceans from the Bay of Bengal to northern Australia, Indonesia and south-eastern Asia. Mostly found inshore and in large estuaries and rivers; some stocks appear to live entirely in fresh water.

A widely dispersed but little-known species, as much at home in the big rivers of southern and south-eastern Asia as in the neighbouring seas. They feed mainly on fish, but also on bottom-living crabs.

Irrawaddy Dolphin

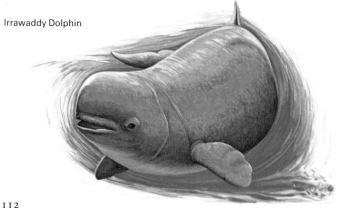

Pygmy Killer Whale   *Feresa attenuata*   (Gray 1875)

SIZE   Nose-to-tail length: males 2.1–2.4 m; females slightly smaller. Weight 150–220 kg.

APPEARANCE   Mainly black, with patches of white or grey about the lips, between the flippers and along the abdomen, broadening about the vent. Tall dorsal fin, slightly recurved; nose rounded, with little or no rostrum. There are 8–11 pairs of stout teeth in the upper jaw, up to 13 pairs in the lower jaw.

RANGE   A species of world-wide distribution in tropical and warm temperate waters; often reported from Japanese waters, suggesting a major concentration in the north-western Pacific Ocean.

Like their larger namesakes, Pygmy Killer Whales seem to be predators of large fish, and possibly of other dolphins, towards which they show aggression in captivity. They hunt in schools of up to fifty. Only rarely are they found close inshore or caught in fishermen's nets.

Pygmy Killer Whale

False Killer Whale

False Killer Whale   *Pseudorca crassidens*   (Owen 1846)

SIZE   Nose-to-tail length: males 4–6 m, females slightly smaller; weight 1–2 tonnes.
APPEARANCE   Slender black whales with little or no grey or white about them. Blunt, rounded face; wide mouth with 8–12 pairs of strong peg-teeth in either jaw. Tall recurving dorsal fin in mid-back.
RANGE   Widely distributed in all but polar seas. Occasionally seen in the Baltic and North Sea, more often in warmer water; mainly an offshore species, though sometimes stranded in large groups.

A widespread but little-known dolphin. Though its size and formidable armoury of teeth suggest larger fare, False Killer Whales seem to feed mainly on fish and cephalopods. They travel in small groups which sometimes unite with large herds; mass strandings have been reported from several coasts where deep water lies close inshore. Few are hunted or caught by fishermen, and little is known of their biology.

Killer Whale   *Orcinus orca*   (Linnaeus 1758)

SIZE   Nose-to-tail length: males 7–10 m, females slightly less; weight 5–7 tonnes.
APPEARANCE   Startlingly black and white: back, sides, tail, fin and flippers black; chin, throat, chest and abdomen white, with a prominent white oval blaze behind the eye, often a grey 'saddle' behind the dorsal fin. Fin tall and upright (to 1.8 m) in old males, tall and recurved in females. Rounded snout; 9–10 pairs of strong peg-like teeth in either jaw.
RANGE   World-wide in every ocean and sea; most common in warm waters far from land, but also known from Arctic and Antarctic waters.

Often regarded as wolves of the sea, Killer Whales move in schools of from three to thirty or forty; surprisingly little is known of their biology, but they are known to eat fish, squid, seals and dolphins, and even to make concerted attacks on whales very much bigger than themselves. Surprising also is their response to captivity; they train easily, jump through hoops with gusto, and demonstrate their affability by allowing their teeth to be brushed with yard-brooms. Calves are about 2 m long at birth. Killer whales are not generally hunted, though a few are taken each year among other dolphins.

Killer Whale

Northern Right Whale Dolphin   *Lissodelphis borealis*   (Peale 1848)

SIZE   Nose-to-tail length 2–3.0 m, males generally larger than females. Weight to about 120 kg.

APPEARANCE   A slender brown or black whale with white patches on the chin, throat and chest, continuing towards the tail in a broad white band. Tail deeply notched, flukes pointed. No dorsal fin. It has 46–48 sharply pointed teeth in either side of upper and lower jaw. Calves pale to dark grey.

RANGE   Widely distributed in temperate waters of the northern Pacific Ocean from Japan to southern California, moving southward and closer inshore in autumn and winter, northward and into deeper water in spring and summer.

A lively and abundant dolphin, often seen in schools of ten to a hundred, occasionally in huge aggregations of two thousand and more. In the eastern Pacific Ocean they gather around islands and banks where squid and fish are plentiful, apparently feeding mostly at the surface.

Southern Right Whale Dolphin   *Lissodelphis peronii*   (Lacépède 1804)

SIZE   Nose-to-tail length 1.5–2.2 m, females slightly smaller than males. Weight about 70 kg.

APPEARANCE   Black or dark grey-brown dorsally, completely white underparts, flippers and flanks. No dorsal fin. It has 40–48 sharp teeth in either side of upper and lower jaw.

RANGE   Circumpolar in cool temperate waters of the Southern Ocean, extending northward in cold currents close to South America, South Africa and New Zealand.

A little-known species of the southern temperate zone, occurring in schools of from twenty to several hundred, often in deep water within sight of land, but also well out to sea. Little is known of its biology.

Commerson's Dolphin   *Cephalorhynchus commersonii*   (Lacépède 1804)

SIZE   Nose-to-tail length 1.4 m; weight about 60 kg.

APPEARANCE   A chubby black and white dolphin; a large white patch extends over most of the sides, flanks, chest and abdomen, leaving black face, fin, dorsal ridge, flippers and tail. It has 25–32 teeth in each half-jaw.

RANGE   Restricted to inshore waters of Argentina from about 42°S to Tierra del Fuego, and southern Chile from about 50°S; also the Falkland Islands, South Georgia and Îles Kerguelen.

A tiny dolphin familiar to sailors in the Falkland Islands and Magellanes regions, though little studied. It moves in small schools of two to four, tumbling slowly through the water and feeding on fish and squid. Its biology is unknown.

Northern Right Whale Dolphin

Southern Right Whale Dolphin

Commerson's Dolphin

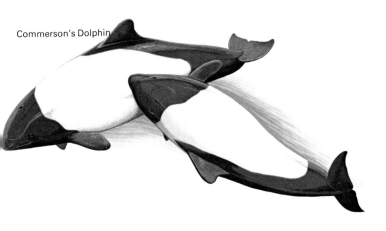

White-bellied (Chilean) Dolphin *Cephalorhynchus eutropia* (Gray 1846)

SIZE   Nose-to-tail length: probably 1–2 m; weight about 50 kg.
APPEARANCE   A small, stocky, almost entirely black dolphin with white patches on the throat, abdomen, and flanks behind the flippers. Teeth: 25–32 in each half-jaw.
RANGE   Restricted to coastal waters of southern Chile, from about 37°S to the Magellanes region and Cape Horn.

Rare and very shy, even in its home waters, this species has seldom been seen and even more rarely photographed or examined, though fishermen in southern Chile occasionally catch it for food or bait.

Heaviside's Dolphin   *Cephalorhynchus heavisidii*   (Gray 1828)

SIZE   Nose-to-tail length: 1–2 m, weight about 50 kg.
APPEARANCE   A blue-black or dark brown dolphin with brilliant white patches on throat, chest and abdomen. The dorsal fin is a broad-based triangle, convex in front and concave behind.
RANGE   Restricted to offshore waters of south-western Africa from the Cape of Good Hope to about 18°S, mostly in the cool Benguela current.

A little-known species of African coastal waters, said to travel in small groups and feed mainly on fish and squid.

Hector's Dolphin   *Cephalorhynchus hectori*   (van Bénéden 1881)

SIZE   Nose-to-tail length 1.2–1.6 m; weight to 55 kg.
APPEARANCE   An elegant little dolphin with black head, tail, fin and flippers, blue-grey or brown flanks and opaque-white throat, chest and abdomen. Very variable colour patterns, but the flippers are usually joined by a dark V-shaped bar, and tapering bars of white usually extend along the flanks. Flippers and dorsal fin rounded, tail flukes long and pointed. Each half-jaw contains 26–32 small pointed teeth.
RANGE   Restricted almost entirely to New Zealand, with possible stragglers to Australia and Borneo. A shallow-water, inshore species of very local distribution.

A small, fast-moving dolphin often seen in groups of three to ten, and occasionally larger herds of a hundred or more, in shallow inshore waters off the east coast of New Zealand. Little is known of its biology. Calving is believed to occur in spring and early summer. Hector's Dolphins eat shallow-water fish and possibly invertebrates from the sea bed. Nobody hunts them, but they are sometimes taken by accident in set nets and trawls, and a few are stranded from time to time. Though possibly numbering only a few thousand, the species seems to be in no danger at present.

White-bellied Dolphin

Heaviside's Dolphin

Hector's Dolphin

Common Dolphin

Common Dolphin *Delphinus delphis* (Linnaeus 1758)

SIZE Nose-to-tail length: males, 2.2–2.6 m, females slightly smaller; weight to about 150 kg.

APPEARANCE Dark slate-grey, black or brown dorsally, with white chin, chest and abdomen, and various patches of yellow and pale grey along the sides and flanks. Dorsal fin tall, with concave leading edge and recurved tip. Rostrum long, slender and sharply delineated from the rounded forehead; 45–50 sharply pointed teeth in each half-jaw.

RANGE A world-wide species of temperate, subtropical and tropical seas, with considerable local variation of colour-pattern; it has already been described under several names, and may well include a dozen or more recognizable geographic races.

A widespread and familiar species, well-known to sailors the world over from its habit of accompanying boats and riding their bow-wave – many dolphins do this, but the Common Dolphin is commoner than most. Schools of a dozen to several hundred have been recorded. They feed on surface-living and deep-water fish and squid, often consorting with schools of tuna in rounding up their prey species. Calves are about 80 cm long at birth; calving is seasonal, at least in temperate latitudes, with spring and autumn peaks. Several thousand Common Dolphins are killed accidentally each year in tuna nets, and many more are hunted for food; up to 120,000 were taken annually in the Black Sea during the 1950s and 60s, until the population collapsed. Elsewhere they are still plentiful – perhaps the most numerous of all the world's dolphins.

Common Dolphin

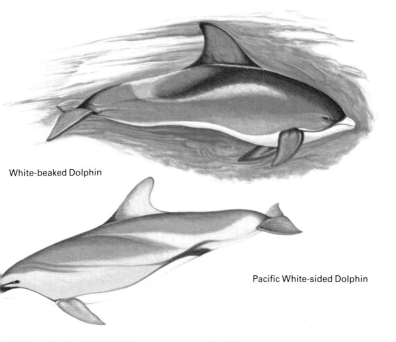

White-beaked Dolphin

Pacific White-sided Dolphin

White-beaked Dolphin *Lagenorhynchus albirostris* (Gray 1846)

SIZE   Nose-to-tail length 2.5–3 m; weight to 270 kg.
APPEARANCE   A large, solidly built dolphin, dark grey to black dorsally with a pale grey patch behind the tall dorsal fin and a grey streak along either side. White face and chin, merging to pale grey chest and abdomen. About 25 small pointed teeth in either half of both jaws.
RANGE   Cool coastal and near-shore waters of the North Atlantic Ocean, from New England to Iceland and western Europe, penetrating north into cold Greenland waters in summer.

A species well-known to North Atlantic fishermen – the high, recurved dorsal fin and white beak are unmistakable. Usually seen in small groups of five to ten, sometimes in association with other species. White-beaked Dolphins feed on surface-living fish and octopus, crustaceans and other shallow-water invertebrates.

Pacific White-sided Dolphin *Lagenorhynchus obliquidens* (Gill 1865)

SIZE   Nose-to-tail length 1.8–2.2 m; weight 120–140 kg.
APPEARANCE   Back and tail black, grading to pale grey. Flanks crossed with white or grey band; chin, chest and underparts white, edged with narrow black band. Tall recurved dorsal fin, dorsal and ventral ridges giving tail a square-cut profile. Tip of chin and flippers black, face mottled grey. Short rostrum with 30–32 sharp teeth in each half-jaw.
RANGE   A species of cool northern Pacific waters, ranging from Kamchatka to Japan in the west and from southern Alaska to Baja California in the east.

This is probably the commonest dolphin of Californian coastal waters, familiar to offshore sailors and fishermen, though less well-known to scientists. They move in schools of a few to several hundred, feeding on fish and squid, staying close to the land in winter but moving out to deeper water in summer. Independent enough to keep well clear of tuna boats, and difficult to drive, they seldom get themselves caught either by accident or by design; a few dozen are caught each year for aquaria, in which they seem to settle quite well.

Dusky Dolphin   *Lagenorhynchus obscurus*   (Gray 1828)

SIZE   Nose-to-tail length 1.8–2.1 m; weight 100–150 kg.
APPEARANCE   Dark grey or black back, shading to grey on the flanks and dorsal fin; white underparts. The grey and the white alternate in complex, very variable patterns on the flanks. Facial patterns variable; often a dark band like a blindfold over rostrum and eyes, continuing as a narrow bridle into the flippers. There are 30–35 small, sharp teeth in each half-jaw.
RANGE   A dolphin of cool, temperate and cold waters of the southern hemisphere, occurring off New Zealand, southern Australia, South America, South Africa and Îles Kerguelen on the Antarctic boundary. An inshore species, possibly with several distinct stocks or geographical races.

Rather rare in comparison with other southern species, Dusky Dolphins occur both in small groups of two to five and in enormous concentrations of several hundred. They feed on fish, gathering around surface shoals, and probably migrate with their food supply. Little is known of their biology.

Atlantic White-sided Dolphin   *Lagenorhynchus acutus*   (Gray 1828)

SIZE   Nose-to-tail length 2.1–3 m; weight about 200 kg.
APPEARANCE   A large dolphin, grey or black above, white below; pale grey flanks streaked with white under the dorsal fin, yellow or brown along the tail. Rostrum broad and short; 30–40 small, sharp teeth in each half-jaw.
RANGE   Cool and cold waters of the northern Atlantic Ocean, ranging from Greenland to New England in the west, and from Scandinavia and Spitzbergen to Britain in the east; common off western Scandinavia and north Britain, rare in the Baltic.

An attractive, colourful dolphin of northern waters, often seen in large schools of over fifty, occasionally in herds of a thousand and more. Mass strandings are occasionally reported in New England and Scandinavia. Atlantic White-sided Dolphins breed in spring and summer, calving after a gestation period of about ten months. They feed on surface-living fish and squid. Though sometimes driven ashore, harpooned or netted with other species, they are too dispersed to suffer seriously from hunting pressures.

Dusky Dolphin

Atlantic White-sided Dolphin

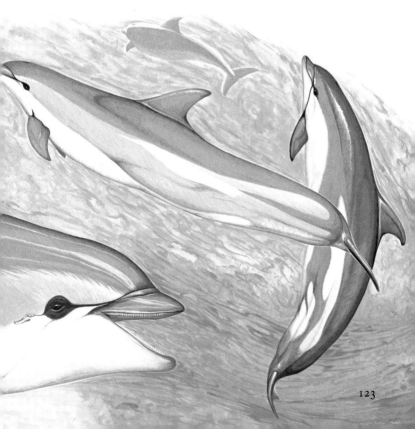

Hourglass Dolphin   *Lagenorhynchus cruciger*   (Quoy and Gaimard 1824)

SIZE   Nose-to-tail length about 2 m; weight about 100 kg.
APPEARANCE   A predominantly black dolphin with white chest and abdomen, and a variable white stripe (sometimes divided into two elongate patches) along the sides from head to tail. Roman profile, with little distinction between rostrum and forehead.
RANGE   Circumpolar in cool and icy waters of the southern oceans.

A rare species, very seldom seen; possibly a distinctive southern variant of the Dusky Dolphin. Nothing is known of its biology.

Peale's Dolphin   *Lagenorhynchus australis*   (Peale 1846)

SIZE   Nose-to-tail length up to 2.1 m; weight 100–140 kg.
APPEARANCE   A dark grey or black dolphin with dark face and back grading to paler sides and flanks; white chest and abdomen; and a distinctive pale longitudinal streak along the upper flank from tall, recurved dorsal fin to the tail. Pointed nose with little or no rostrum.
RANGE   Restricted to near-shore waters of southern South America, mostly below 40°S, and the Falkland Islands.

A dolphin of restricted distribution, though probably not rare. Nothing is known of its biology.

Melon-headed Dolphin   *Peponocephala electra*   (Gray 1846)

SIZE   Nose-to-tail length: males 2.4–2.8 m; females slightly smaller.
APPEARANCE   A slender dark-grey-to-black dolphin with white lips and variable patches of pale grey underneath. Rounded 'melon' head with little or no beak. There are about 21–25 small teeth in each half-jaw. Strongly recurved dorsal fin close to the midpoint of the body; flippers long and pointed.
RANGE   Warm temperate and tropical waters of the Pacific and Atlantic Oceans.

A rather rare and little-known species. Melon-headed Dolphins appear to live in large schools of several hundred individuals and occasionally get stranded on beaches as far apart as Japan and Australia. Little or nothing is known of their biology.

Hourglass Dolphin

Peale's Dolphin

Melon-headed Dolphin

Fraser's Dolphin *Lagenodelphis hosei* (Fraser 1956)

SIZE   Nose-to-tail length 2.2–2.6 m; males possibly slightly larger than females; weight about 100 kg.

APPEARANCE   Dark grey-blue with a brown cast on back, tail, fin and flippers, grading to paler blue on the sides; a broad lateral stripe of dark grey, white chin, chest and abdomen. Dark bridle edged with blue between eye and flipper. Dorsal fin short, recurved; tail flukes long and slender. There are 39–44 sharply pointed teeth in each half-jaw.

RANGE   A tropical dolphin so far reported sparsely from Sarawak, the eastern Pacific, off South Africa and south-eastern Australia; possibly rare and restricted to the Indian and Pacific Oceans.

Until 1970 this species was known only from a single specimen, washed up on a beach in Malaya in 1895 and formally described and listed in 1956. It has since been rediscovered in three widely separated areas of the Indian and Pacific Oceans. Fraser's Dolphin seems in many ways to be intermediate between *Lagenorhynchus* and *Delphinus* dolphins, with some of the characteristics of both – hence its Latin name. It seems to swim in small groups, often in association with other species; very little is so far known of its biology.

Spinner Dolphin *Stenella longirostris* (Gray 1828)

SIZE   Nose-to-tail length 1.8–2.2 m, possibly more in some of the larger stocks; weight 70–90 kg.

APPEARANCE   Dark grey-brown dorsally, grading to paler grey or white underneath, and splashed with darker spots. Large dark dorsal fin, dark flippers and tail. The rostrum is long, with 40 or more small teeth in each half-jaw.

RANGE   A dolphin of tropical offshore and deep inshore waters, distributed worldwide. Previously reported under several names, this species probably includes many distinctive stocks and races.

Named from their habit of leaping from the water and corkscrewing through the air, Spinner Dolphins are well-known to offshore fishermen in many parts of the world. They feed on schooling fish and squid, often well below the surface layer of the ocean; hunting frequently with schools of tuna and other large predators, they are good indicators to fishermen that the fish are about. Many thousands die each year, along with Pacific Spotted Dolphins, in seine nets set for tuna. Though usually able to avoid set nets, they seem unable to find their way out of a closing seine, becoming entangled and drowning. Efforts are being made to provide escape hatches in the nets; playing recordings of Killer Whales also helps to drive the dolphins away. Most births occur in spring and autumn, at least in some stocks. Calves are about 80 cm long at birth.

Striped (Euphrosyne) Dolphin *Stenella coeruleoalba* (Meyen 1833)

SIZE   Nose-to-tail length: males 2.1–2.5 m, females 2.1–2.3 m; weight about 100 kg.

APPEARANCE   An elegant grey and blue dolphin, with white chin, throat and chest crossed by a pattern of grey or brownish stripes. Forty or more small teeth in each half-jaw.

Fraser's Dolphin

Long-beaked
(Spinner) Dolphin

Striped Dolphin

RANGE   Widely distributed in tropical and temperate waters of all the oceans; mainly a deep-water species though often found close inshore. Several geographical stocks or races may be distinguishable.

This is a highly sociable species of warm tropical waters, which lives in large schools of thirty to forty and often aggregates into herds of several hundred. Schooling fish and squid are its main food. The big herds, vulnerable to hunting, are often driven ashore or netted, especially in Japan where Striped Dolphins migrate close inshore each winter. Studies there have shown that mating and calving occur in most months, though with seasonal peaks. Gestation takes a year; the calves are 1 m long at birth, and 1.6 m by the time they are weaned at the end of their first year. Both sexes mature at eight or nine years, and cows thereafter produce a calf every second or third year. These dolphins live as long as fifty years. Heavy hunting – up to 20,000 dolphins per year – has taken its toll of Japanese stocks, though the world population as a whole is unlikely to be affected. Elsewhere small numbers are caught accidentally in set nets and tuna-fishing operations.

Pacific Spotted Dolphin   *Stenella attenuata*   (Gray 1846)

SIZE   Nose-to-tail length: males of largest stocks 2.0–2.5 m, females 1.6–2.2 m; other forms 10–20 per cent smaller. Weight of large males 100–115 kg.
APPEARANCE   A slender, streamlined dolphin, blue-black dorsally and grey dappled with spots on flanks and abdomen. White cheeks with dark eye-stripe; narrow rostrum and chin, in some stocks tipped with white. Dorsal fin strongly recurved, slender pointed flippers. There are 41–45 small pointed teeth in each half-jaw.
RANGE   Widespread in all the warm oceans; best-known from the Pacific, but the same species is believed to be present in the Indian and Atlantic Oceans as well. There are many local variations of colour and size.

Pacific Spotted Dolphin

A fairly common species of wide distribution in the Pacific, almost certainly warranting division into several geographic races. They feed on squid and surface-living fish, including flying fish. Like others of their genus these dolphins often associate with tuna, and many tens of thousands are killed accidentally each year in tuna-fishing operations. A few hundred are taken annually off Japan. About 90 cm long at birth, the calves grow to 1.4 m in their first year and then more slowly to reach full size between the ages of eight and ten. Gestation takes a year, lactation possibly two years, so cows are believed to calve every fourth year. Spotted Dolphins probably live for forty to forty-five years.

Atlantic Spotted Dolphin *Stenella plagiodon* (Cope 1866) (not illustrated)

SIZE   Nose-to-tail length: about 2 m; weight 100–120 kg.
APPEARANCE   A dark blue-grey dolphin with paler flanks and abdomen, heavily spotted and flecked.
RANGE   Reported only from the south-eastern coast of the United States.

A little-known species, superficially at least very much like the Pacific Spotted Dolphin.

Bottlenose Dolphin *Tursiops truncatus* (Montagu 1821)

SIZE   Nose-to-tail length 2.5–3 m, up to 4 m in larger stocks; weight about 200 kg.
APPEARANCE   Large, cheerful-looking dolphins, silver-grey above and paler grey below, with considerable local variation. About 20 strong pointed teeth in each half-jaw.
RANGE   A coastal and near-shore species of temperate and tropical oceans all over the world. Several separate stocks or races may exist. Those of cool waters tend to be larger than warm-water forms.

Of almost world-wide distribution, and familiar for their performance in show-business, these are most people's idea of what a dolphin should be. Surprisingly little is known of their natural life. They live in small groups of a few to several dozen, feeding on shallow-water fish. Females probably mature at five or more years old and produce calves every second year. Calves are 1–1.2 m long at birth; those that survive the first few difficult years of life may live for twenty-five or thirty years. Intensely sociable, Bottlenose Dolphins have from time to time made friends with swimmers, showing themselves

Bottlenose Dolphin

playful, intelligent and curious. They live well in captivity, readily learning certain kinds of tricks and being usually happy to perform them.

Risso's Dolphin *Grampus griseus* (Cuvier 1812)

SIZE   Nose-to-tail length: 3.0–4.0 m; weight up to 650 kg or more.
APPEARANCE   A large dark, square-cut dolphin with thick body and ridged tail. Dark grey back, paler grey flanks and underparts. Large forehead almost overhanging the rostrum. Tall recurved dorsal fin, broad tail flukes, narrow pointed flippers. No functional teeth in the upper jaw; up to a dozen small pointed teeth in the front of the lower jaw.
RANGE   Widely distributed in temperate and warm seas, recorded in the south from New Zealand, Argentina and South Africa, and in the north from the Kuril Islands, British Columbia, Newfoundland, southern Scandinavia, Britain and the North Sea coast.

A solitary or only mildly sociable species, rather rare and seldom seen in large groups, though widespread about the world. Calves are about 1.5 m long at birth. Risso's Dolphins feed mainly on cephalopods, for which they are believed to dive deep; the saying 'puffing like a grampus' reflects the quick, deep breathing needed to get their breath back after a long dive. Though not often sociable with man or his ships, 'Pelorus Jack' – a large male Risso's Dolphin of New Zealand – accompanied the Wellington–Nelson ferry through Pelorus Sound almost every day for twenty-four years.

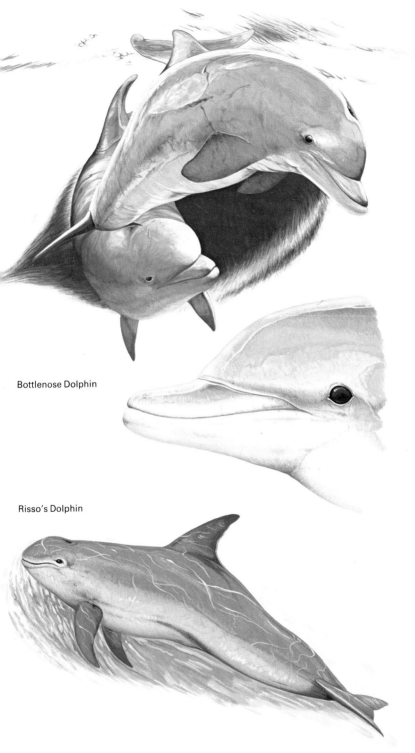

Bottlenose Dolphin

Risso's Dolphin

SUBORDER MYSTICETI

There are ten species of whalebone whales, here listed in three families. Their most striking common feature is an absence of teeth in adults (embryo mysticetes sometimes have tiny non-functional ones) and the presence instead of whalebone (baleen) plates – in some species over 300 a side – hanging from the roof of the mouth. The skull is symmetrical, with both nostrils always functional; all the ribs are single-headed and rather loosely hinged to the vertebrae, and the flippers often have a reduced number of fingers – though many more finger-joints in compensation.

Baleen is a horny material similar to hair or fingernails, growing in triangular plates 0.5 cm thick and up to 3 m long. Hanging just over 1 cm apart at a right angle to the main axis of the whale, with the shortest at the front and longest in the rear, the plates form a filter through which sea water is strained. Their efficiency is improved by fraying; while the outer edges of the plates are smooth, the inner edges are frayed into criss-crossing strands. The three families of mysticete whales filter in slightly different ways. Standing inside the mouth of a Right Whale (as a dozen people can together) is like standing in a Gothic arcade floored with tongue and lined with fine coconut matting. From a continuous flow of plankton-rich sea water the small animals are filtered and left behind on the matting, to be swept backward down the throat. Fin and Grey Whales have shorter baleen; only the roof of the mouth is matted. They take in discrete mouthfuls of sea water and strain out larger particles of food by pressure through a much coarser filter.

FAMILY BALAENIDAE

This small family includes the three species of right whales, so-called because they are slow-moving and were easily caught by old-time open-boat whalers, when baleen was the main prize. They often migrated close to the shore, and pregnant cows came into shallow, sheltered bays to produce their calves. Right whales were also well endowed with oil, and buoyant enough to remain afloat after harpooning. Distinguishing characters include the enormous head with arched lower lips, lack of a dorsal fin in the larger species, a smooth (ungrooved) throat, and sensory whiskers on the face.

FAMILY BALAENIDAE

Subfamily Balaeninae
Balaena glacialis (3 races)   Black Right Whale
Balaena mysticetus   Greenland Right (Bowhead)
                                       Whale
Caperea marginata   Pygmy Right Whale

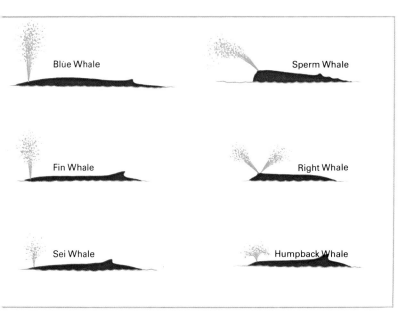

Spouts and dorsal fins of various whales

Black Right Whale   *Balaena glacialis*   (Müller 1776)

SIZE   Nose-to-tail length 14–15.5 m: southern stocks may be slightly larger than northern; weight 50–100 tonnes.

APPEARANCE   A large, fat whale with a very deep lower jaw covering baleen plates up to 2.5 m long. The top of the head and back form a continuous unbroken line. Black on dark brown, with grey or white abdominal markings; patches of pale, rough, horny skin decorate the face, including a 'bonnet' on the tip of the nose.

RANGE   World-wide in temperate and cool seas; oceanic, but cows often enter shallow water to give birth. Three geographical races are distinguished: (i) *E.g. glacialis* of the northern Atlantic Ocean; (ii) *E.g. japonica* of the northern Pacific; and (iii) *E.g. australis* of the southern oceans, which is often regarded as a separate species, *E. australis*; all three forms are very similar.

This species is found sparsely in temperate oceans all over the world from Newfoundland, Norway and the Aleutian Islands to South America and Australia. Several local stocks are identified; others may have existed in the past; but Black Right Whales have been hunted for centuries wherever they appeared and, despite almost world-wide protection since 1935, they have not fully recovered. Usually solitary or in groups of two to five, they feed by swimming close to the sea surface with mouth open, skimming off very fine plankton as they go. Calves are born in early spring after a gestation period of a year or more, measuring 6 m. Little is known of the biology of this species in northern waters; southern stocks are rather better known, though most of the hunting was over before scientific studies could be made.

133

Greenland Right (Bowhead) Whale *Balaena mysticetus* (Linnaeus 1758)

SIZE   Nose-to-tail length to 18 m; weight about 100 tonnes.

APPEARANCE   A mainly black whale, large and fat, with a white patch on the chin and lower jaw, sometimes extending to the upper jaw; the white is often tinged yellow by a diatom film. Distinct bump on top of head.

RANGE   Arctic Ocean and neighbouring seas; seen off Spitzbergen, Jan Mayen, Greenland, and in the Bering Sea. Probably several discrete geographical stocks.

Slightly larger than the Black Right Whale, this species inhabits north polar seas. With up to 300 baleen plates on either side, the longest 2.5 m long, it was especially prized by early whalers and hunted almost to extinction during the eighteenth and nineteenth centuries. The small stocks remaining are now protected, except that Eskimos are allowed to take a few each year. Pacific stocks seem to be recovering well and may have stabilized; this is still a very rare species in the north Atlantic. Greenland Right Whales (known as Bowheads in Alaska) are reported to mate in late summer while in high latitudes. They swim south into sub-polar waters as the winter ice forms, and there give birth to their calves in early spring after a gestation period of about sixteen months.

Pygmy Right Whale   *Caperea marginata*   (Gray 1846)

SIZE   Nose-to-tail length 5–6.2 m; weight 4–5 tonnes.

APPEARANCE   In general shape a miniature version of the larger right whales, though with a small, slightly recurved dorsal fin and proportionately smaller mouth. Black or dark grey above, paler below, with mainly white baleen.

RANGE   A species of southern temperate waters, found off New Zealand, Australia, South America and South Africa.

Greenland Right Whale

Black Right Whale

135

This whale is known from occasional strandings and captures at sea; too small and dispersed to be worth hunting, it has attracted little scientific attention. It moves in schools of six to eight, sometimes associating with other whales, and feeds by filtering small crustaceans. Pygmy Right Whales seem to come closer to shore, and therefore be more liable to stranding, during spring and summer when plankton is most plentiful.

FAMILY ESCHRICHTIDAE

This tiny family contains only one living species – the Grey Whale of the northern Pacific Ocean. In some ways intermediate between right whales and rorquals, Grey Whales have about 150 short baleen plates on either side, one or two pairs of grooves on the throat, and a row of small humps along the tail ridge, the first and largest resembling a dorsal fin. Up to the early eighteenth century there were Grey Whales in the northern Atlantic Ocean too. Present on both eastern and western shores, stocks seem even then to have been small and on the point of disappearing, and no more than helped on their way by the early European and New England whalers.

FAMILY ESCHRICHTIDAE

Subfamily Eschrichtinae
  Eschrichtius gibbosus   Grey Whale

Grey Whale   *Eschrichtius gibbosus*   (Erxleben 1777)

SIZE   Nose-to-tail length 12–16 m, females slightly larger than males; weight 25–30 tonnes.
APPEARANCE   A long grey whale with slightly curved mouth, broad pointed flippers and small hump in position of dorsal fin. Often barnacle-covered. Slow and deliberate in its movements. Two to four short grooves in the throat. Short white baleen.
RANGE   Northern Pacific Ocean and Bering Sea. Eastern stocks move south to southern and Baja California, western stocks to Japan and Korea.

A well-known species of Pacific coastal waters, currently staging a come-back after severe hunting. From the tiny population remaining in 1937, when full international protection was given, the species has now built up substantial numbers. Groups of four to seven can often be seen from the Californian beaches from November to March, heading southward to the warm waters of Baja California. There the eastern stocks winter and pregnant cows give birth to their calves. In spring they migrate northward again, this time well out from the coast and heading for the rich feeding grounds of the Bering and neighbouring seas. Western stocks similarly winter near Korea and spend summers in the Sea of Okhotsk. They cruise slowly at 6–8 km per hour; during courtship on their summer grounds they race and gambol like dolphins, leaping from the water and landing spectacularly on their backs. Grey Whales are filter feeders, especially at the northern end of their range, where they take plankton and small fish. In southern coastal waters they are reported also to scrape or suck food from the mud of the sea floor.

Pygmy Right Whale

Grey Whale

FAMILY BALAENOPTERIDAE

This family includes five species of rorquals or 'pleated' whales, all in a single genus (*Balaenoptera*), and a sixth closely related but distinct species – the Humpback – in a genus (*Megaptera*) of its own. Rorquals are long, slender whales, streamlined and fast-moving, with flattened head, pointed flippers, a small, recurved dorsal fin set well back along the body, and from sixty to eighty grooves or pleats running longitudinally along the throat, chest and abdomen. Blue Whales are the largest, sometimes exceeding 30 m; Fin Whales are slightly smaller at 20–25 m, Sei and Bryde's Whales smaller still at 10–15 m, and Minke Whales are relatively tiny, seldom exceeding 10 m. Humpback Whales share the rorquals' basic characteristics of grooved ventral surface and recurved dorsal fin, but their pleats are much coarser and they lack the rorquals' elegant lines. Built for comfort rather than speed, they have immensely long flippers and a rugged, bumpy skin. Old-time whalers saw Humpbacks as cheerful clowns, with a liking for leaping and tumbling in the water; rorquals – even the smaller ones – were much more serious-minded prey.

FAMILY BALAENOPTERIDAE

Subfamily Balaenopterinae

Balaenoptera musculus	Blue Whale
Balaenoptera physalus	Fin Whale
Balaenoptera borealis	Sei Whale
Balaenoptera edeni	Bryde's Whale
Balaenoptera acutorostrata	Minke (Piked) Whale
Megaptera novaeangliae	Humpback Whale

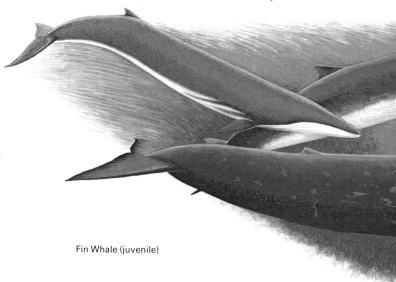

Fin Whale (juvenile)

Blue Whale   *Balaenoptera musculus*   (Linnaeus 1758)

SIZE   Nose-to-tail length 25–33 m; females average slightly larger than males, and southern Blue Whales tend to be longer than northern ones. Weight 100–120 tonnes in full fat; the record is about 180 tonnes.

APPEARANCE   Enormous all-grey mottled whale, sometimes grey-blue because of a yellow film of surface diatoms. Flippers slender and pointed, with pale grey tips and undersurface. Dorsal fin small, recurved, set four fifths of the way back along the body.

RANGE   Cosmopolitan in all oceans. There are geographically isolated populations in the north Pacific, north Atlantic and southern hemisphere, each divisible into semi-separate stocks which migrate longitudinally. 'Pygmy Blue Whales' are a stock of the southern Indian Ocean, about three quarters of the size of normal ones but otherwise similar; some authorities regard them as a distinct subspecies.

These splendid animals were formerly abundant in offshore waters all over the world. After the development of the explosive harpoon in the late nineteenth century their size and high yield of oil made them the prime target of whalers, especially of the highly mechanized pelagic whaling fleets operating in polar waters, where the fattest whales were found. Now Blue Whales are seldom seen; only some 12,000–15,000 are left from stocks which must originally have numbered hundreds of thousands. Like Fin Whales they winter in warm temperate and tropical waters, where the calves (7 m long, 2.5 tonnes) are born and mating occurs. In spring they move polewards, singly or in groups of two or three. The calves are weaned at seven months (16 m, 25 tonnes). Penetrating well inside the pack-ice they fatten on the rich summer plankton. In autumn they head back towards the tropics, laden with stocks of blubber that will see them through the lean months in warmer waters. Cows mature at about five years and breed every second or third year; lifespan for

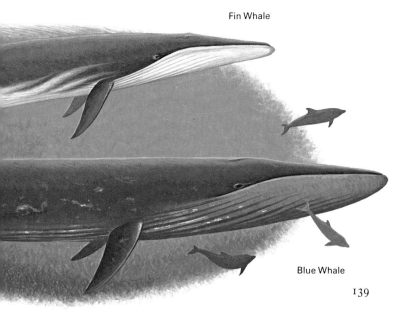

Fin Whale

Blue Whale

either sex is sixty to eighty years. There are hopes that under continuing protection their stocks will recover. Blue Whales feed by engulfing huge mouthfuls of plankton-rich water and pressing out the plankton – mostly krill a few centimetres long – on their baleen filter; in summer they are estimated to take 3–4 tonnes daily.

Fin Whale   *Balaenoptera physalus*   (Linnaeus 1758)

SIZE   Nose-to-tail length 20–25 m; females tend to be larger than males, and southern Fin Whales are 5–10 per cent larger than northern ones; weight about 40 tonnes.
APPEARANCE   Large silvery to slate-grey whales with white underparts, including the undersurface of the flippers; the right lower jaw and the baleen above it are white. Tall recurved dorsal fin set three quarters of the way back along the body.
RANGE   A species of the deep offshore waters, widespread in the Pacific, Atlantic and Indian Oceans; penetrates far north and south, though seldom found beyond the ice edge. Several separate stocks have been identified.

Second largest of the rorquals, Fin Whales have a world-wide distribution, though individuals seem to live in small groups with fairly restricted migratory pathways. Annual cycles have been worked out most fully in southern stocks; northern stocks probably live in much the same way. Autumn finds them heading towards temperate or tropical waters, where cows give birth to their calves in May and June. Born 6–7 m long, the calves suckle and grow rapidly; by July and August they are big enough to be starting the long journey that takes them south into polar waters. Fin Whales feed by engulfing plankton and small fish; there is some evidence that they concentrate the shoals by circling round them, then charge through taking huge gulps as they go. Heavily hunted both from shore stations and by the pelagic fleets, their numbers are much reduced. Only a few thousand remain in the north Pacific and Atlantic Oceans, and a few tens of thousands in the Southern Ocean; the larger stocks are still subject to hunting, under quotas determined each year.

Sei Whale   *Balaenoptera borealis*   (Lesson 1828)

SIZE   Nose-to-tail length 10–17 m; the largest are often females. Weight about 15 tonnes.
APPEARANCE   A slender blue-black whale with a varying band of white underneath – narrow at the chin and throat, broadening at the abdomen. Thirty to sixty grooves on the throat, extending as far back as the tips of the flippers; fin tall, about two thirds of the way along the body. Baleen fine, mostly black.
RANGE   Widely distributed in all the oceans; found in temperate and tropical waters throughout the year, and migrating into cooler waters in summer.

A wide-ranging species, formerly plentiful in deep offshore waters but now much rarer due to commercial hunting. Much smaller than Blue or Fin Whales (though still larger than any land mammal), with a relatively low yield of oil, Sei Whales were caught only in small numbers while the big rorquals were plentiful; their stocks may even have increased as the whalers took more and more of their larger competitors. But their turn for being killed came in the late 1940s, and from then onward Seis increasingly helped to support the industry. Part of their attraction is their meat, which is well-favoured in Japan. Sei Whales migrate between warm temperate or tropical waters in winter and cool temperate to cold waters – even to the ice edge – in summer. Usually travelling in small groups, they occasionally form gatherings of fifty or more where food is plentiful. Calves are about 3 m long at birth, and cows are believed to give birth every second or third year. As their very fine baleen suggests, Sei Whales feed mainly on tiny copepods, which they skim in mouthfuls from the surface of the ocean.

Sei Whale

Bryde's Whale   *Balaenoptera edeni*   (Anderson 1878)

SIZE   Nose-to-tail length 10–14 m; females tend to be larger than males. Weight about 15 tonnes.
APPEARANCE   Closely resembles the Sei Whale in size, shape and dorsal colouring. However, the throat and chest are mostly grey, and the ventral grooves extend further back along the abdomen to the level of the navel. The baleen is coarse and short, white in the front of the jaw and grey or black at the back.
RANGE   Tropical and warm temperate waters of the Atlantic and Indian Oceans; also in New Zealand and Japanese waters of the western Pacific Ocean. There are several distinct stocks.

A fairly common whale of the tropics, this species is a warm-water counterpart of the Sei Whale, seldom if ever found in sub-polar or even cold temperate seas. It is best known from South African waters, where several hundred are taken each year, and also from Japan and other north Pacific stations. Like the Sei it was of little interest to commercial hunters until Blue and Fin Whales became scarce. Its baleen is much coarser than that of the Sei Whale, indicating a diet of larger plankton and fish; Bryde's Whales have been seen hunting among fish shoals off South Africa, even taking penguins which happened to be there at the same time. They reach sexual maturity at seven to eight years and full size at fifteen to sixteen years. Little is known of their breeding, but cows probably produce a calf at best every second year.

Minke (Piked) Whale   *Balaenoptera acutorostrata*   (Lacépède 1804)

SIZE   Nose-to-tail length up to 9 m, females slightly smaller; weight 5–9 tonnes.
APPEARANCE   Small dark grey or black rorquals with paler underparts and sides; the flippers have a distinctive white bar in northern stocks, and are mainly white in some southern stocks. Prominent, recurved dorsal fin set well back towards the tail. Sharply ridged rostrum; about sixty throat grooves.
RANGE   Temperate waters of both hemispheres; many males and immature females migrate into sub-polar and polar seas – even among the ice – in summer. Several local stocks are identified.

Smallest of the rorquals, Minke Whales live mainly in small groups of five to ten in cool or cold waters; their food includes krill and small fish. They have been hunted in the northern hemisphere for over fifty years, mostly from shore stations; pelagic whalers bothered them little while good stocks of larger rorquals remained. But with the demise of the Blue, Fin and Sei Whales, Minkes now bear the main pressure of hunting, and several thousand are killed each year in both hemispheres. Calves are born in the warmer waters of their range, measuring 2.8 m, after a gestation period of ten to eleven months. Mating occurs over a long season from late winter to early summer.

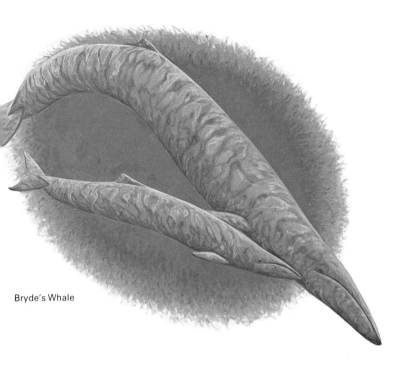

Bryde's Whale

Minke Whale

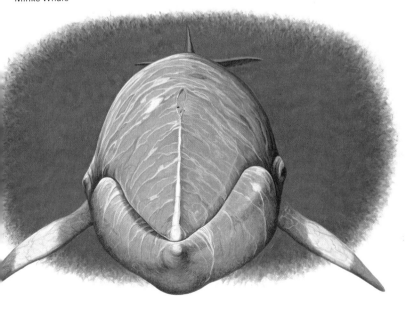

Humpback Whale *Megaptera novaeangliae* (Borowski 1781)

SIZE Nose-to-tail length 15–17 m; weight about 35 tonnes.

APPEARANCE A fat black or dark-grey whale with irregular white patches on abdomen and tail, coarse pleats on throat and abdomen, dorsal fin two thirds of the way along the back and followed by a series of bumps; long knobbly flippers.

RANGE A widespread species of all the oceans, living mainly offshore but tending to hug the coast during migration. Separate stocks are identified on either side of the northern Pacific and Atlantic Oceans, and in five or more sectors of the Southern Ocean.

Formerly an abundant species in every ocean, Humpbacks are whales of character – lively, noisy and pleasantly ugly with their ungainly proportions, warts, bumps, and barnacle-encrusted skins. Like camels they look as though they were designed by a committee, but are obviously well-equipped for their slow, easy-going role in the oceans of the world. Well-known acrobats, they hurl themselves out of the water in courtship display, flinging their tails – often piebald and tattered – into the air before diving. However, their slow speed and inshore migration routes made them easy prey for whalers, and now there are very few left in the world. Like other mysticetes they migrate north and south, wintering in the tropics where they produce their calves, and spending summers in sub-polar or polar seas. They feed on fish and krill; Humpbacks have been seen to make shallow, spiral dives under a shoal of food, setting up a curtain of bubbles which contain and concentrate the prey, and so make them easier to engulf.

Distribution Maps

Africa

⊙ Tristan da Cunha
⊙ Gough I.

South America

South Georgia
South Sandwich Is.

⊙ Marion I.

South Orkney Is.

⊙ Îles Crozet

South Shetland Is.

⊙ Kerguelen
⊙ Heard I.

Antarctica

⊙ Macquarie I.
Campbell I. ⊙
Antipodes Is. ⊙

Australia

New Zealand

········· Weddell Seal
— · — Ross and Crabeater Seals
———— Southern Elephant Seal breeding areas

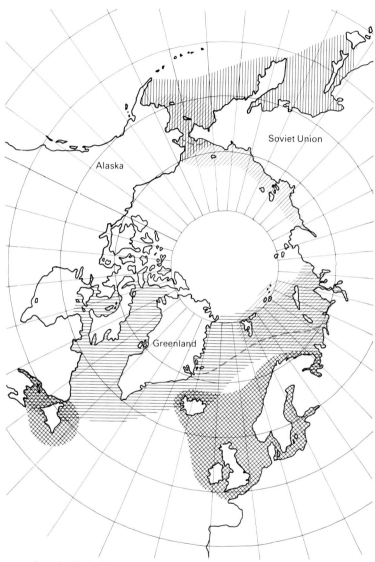

Soviet Union

Alaska

Greenland

— — — Breeding limit of Polar Bears

Walrus

Ribbon Seal

Harp Seal

Grey Seal

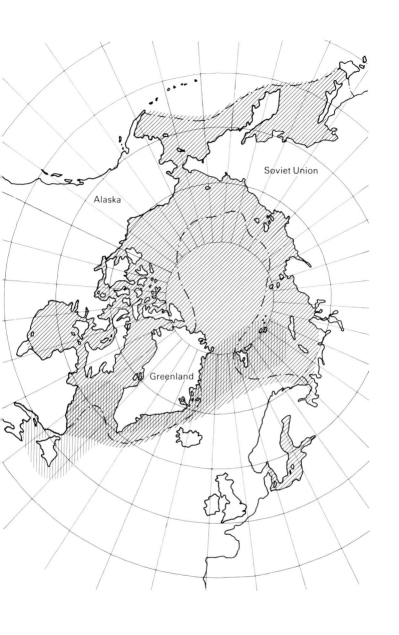

Soviet Union

Alaska

Greenland

 — · — Breeding limit of Bearded Seal

Ringed Seal

Hooded Seal

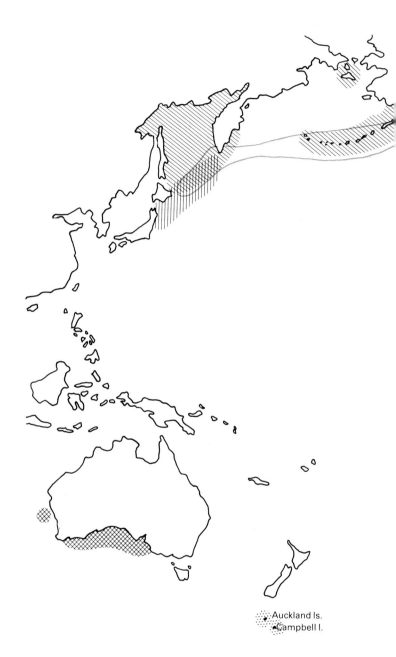

Auckland Is.
Campbell I.

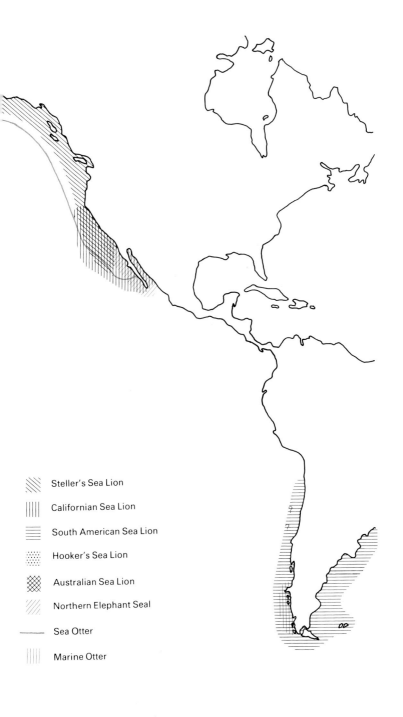

Steller's Sea Lion

Californian Sea Lion

South American Sea Lion

Hooker's Sea Lion

Australian Sea Lion

Northern Elephant Seal

Sea Otter

Marine Otter

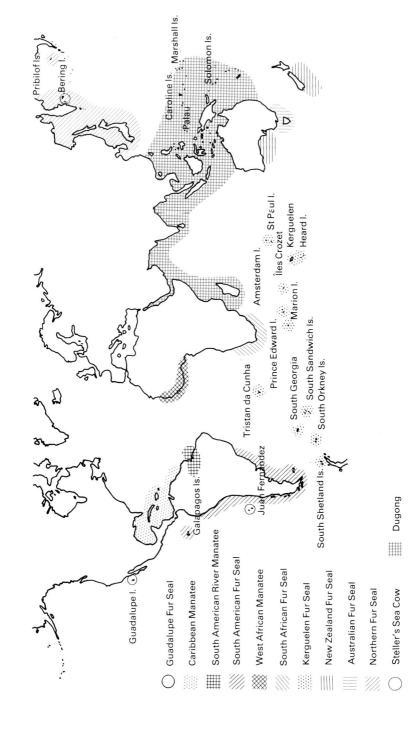

Pribilof Is.
Bering I.

Caroline Is.   Marshall Is.
Palau
Solomon Is.

St Paul I.
Amsterdam I.
Îles Crozet   Kerguelen
Heard I.

Prince Edward I.
Marion I.

South Georgia
South Sandwich Is.
South Orkney Is.

Tristan da Cunha

Guadalupe I.

Galápagos Is.
Juan Fernández

South Shetland Is.

Guadalupe Fur Seal
Caribbean Manatee
South American River Manatee
South American Fur Seal
West African Manatee
South African Fur Seal
Kerguelen Fur Seal
New Zealand Fur Seal
Australian Fur Seal
Northern Fur Seal

Steller's Sea Cow   Dugong

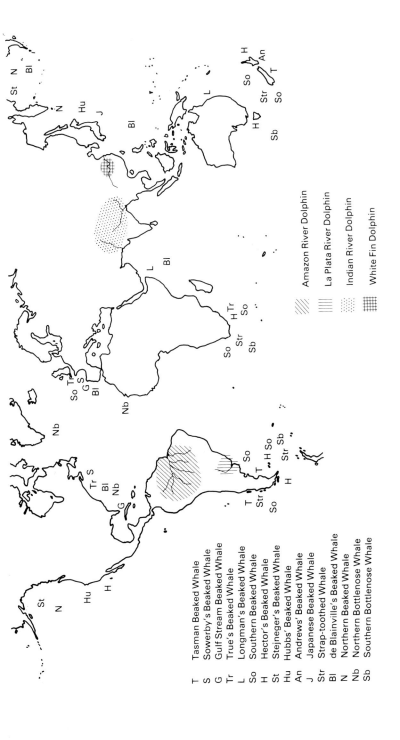

T   Tasman Beaked Whale
S   Sowerby's Beaked Whale
G   Gulf Stream Beaked Whale
Tr   True's Beaked Whale
L   Longman's Beaked Whale
So   Southern Beaked Whale
H   Hector's Beaked Whale
St   Steinger's Beaked Whale
Hu   Hubbs' Beaked Whale
An   Andrews' Beaked Whale
J   Japanese Beaked Whale
Str   Strap-toothed Whale
Bl   de Blainville's Beaked Whale
N   Northern Beaked Whale
Nb   Northern Bottlenose Whale
Sb   Southern Bottlenose Whale

Amazon River Dolphin

La Plata River Dolphin

Indian River Dolphin

White Fin Dolphin

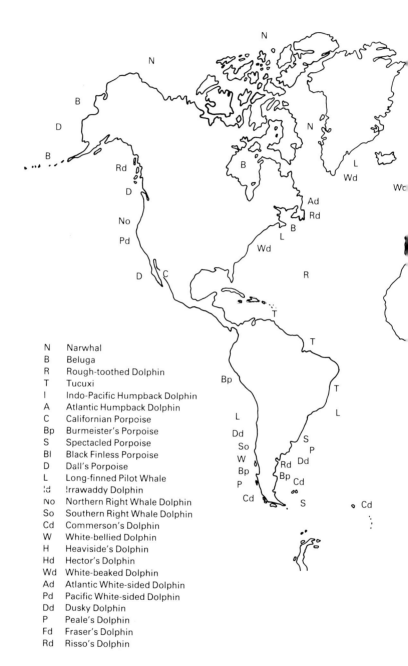

N	Narwhal
B	Beluga
R	Rough-toothed Dolphin
T	Tucuxi
I	Indo-Pacific Humpback Dolphin
A	Atlantic Humpback Dolphin
C	Californian Porpoise
Bp	Burmeister's Porpoise
S	Spectacled Porpoise
Bl	Black Finless Porpoise
D	Dall's Porpoise
L	Long-finned Pilot Whale
Id	Irrawaddy Dolphin
No	Northern Right Whale Dolphin
So	Southern Right Whale Dolphin
Cd	Commerson's Dolphin
W	White-bellied Dolphin
H	Heaviside's Dolphin
Hd	Hector's Dolphin
Wd	White-beaked Dolphin
Ad	Atlantic White-sided Dolphin
Pd	Pacific White-sided Dolphin
Dd	Dusky Dolphin
P	Peale's Dolphin
Fd	Fraser's Dolphin
Rd	Risso's Dolphin

Further reading

Bonner, W. N., *Whales*, Poole (Dorset), Blandford Press, 1980.

Brown, S. G., 'A review of Antarctic whaling', in *Polar Record* 11, 1963, pp. 555–66.

Burton, R. W., *The Life and Death of Whales*, London, André Deutsch, 1973.

Gaskin, D. E., *The Ecology of Whales and Dolphins*, London, Heinemann, 1982.

Harrison, R. J., and King, J. E., *Marine Mammals*, London, Hutchinson, 1980.

Harrison, R. J., ed., *Functional Anatomy of Marine Mammals*, London, Academic Press, 1974 –.

Hewer, H. R., *British Seals*, London, Collins, 1974.

King, J. E., *Seals of the World*, London, British Museum (Natural History), 1964.

Mackintosh, N. A., *The Stocks of Whales*, Farnham (Surrey), Fishing News (Books) Ltd, 1965.

Matthews, L. H., *The Natural History of the Whale*, London, Weidenfeld & Nicolson, 1978.

Norris, K. S., ed., *Whales, Dolphins and Porpoises*, Berkeley, University of California Press, 1966.

Scheffer, V. B., *Seals, Sea Lions and Walruses; a Review of the Pinnipedia*, Stanford, Stanford University Press, 1958.

Slijper, E. J., *Whales*, London, Hutchinson, 1962.

Watson, L., *Sea Guide to Whales of the World*, London, Hutchinson, 1981.

INDEX

Penguin Books
Sea Mammals of the World

Dr Bernard Stonehouse trained as a biologist at University College, London, and Merton College, Oxford. For most of his career he has worked on the ecology of polar and sub-polar regions, with special interests in marine birds and mammals of the far south; he has spent four winters and many summers in the Antarctic with British and New Zealand expeditions. While on the staff of the Edward Grey Institute, University of Oxford, he led the British Ornithologists' Union Centenary Expedition to Ascension Island, studying the reproductive rhythms of seabirds near the equator. Later he became Reader in Zoology at the University of Canterbury, New Zealand, where he led research on introduced mammals, seals and whales – research which extended south to the sub-Antarctic islands and Antarctica. As a visiting professor at Yale University and Canadian Commonwealth Research Fellow in the University of British Columbia, Canada, he worked on northern mammals, paying several visits to the Yukon. Dr Stonehouse holds the Polar Medal for services in Antarctica, the Union Medal of the British Ornithologists' Union for long-term ornithological research and the Voyce Trophy of the New Zealand Antarctic Society for conservation work in Antarctica. Author of many research papers and books, he has also edited research symposia and other scientific volumes for several publishers. For some time Chairman of the Postgraduate School of Studies in Environmental Science at the University of Bradford, he is currently at the Scott Polar Research Institute, University of Cambridge.

For Martin Camm, an early interest in angling developed and encouraged a general love for all aspects of our natural world. His talent for drawing enabled him to express something of his fascination and delight, and, following college courses at Grimsby and Camberwell, he moved straight into the field of natural history illustration with books on bird and fish identification. Working hard on launching a professional career, however, did not prevent him from finding time to return to the riverbank. Here in the countryside the changes wrought by new farming methods, pollution and the pressures of modern society are obvious to a disciplined eye, particularly as they merely reflect what is happening on a global scale. When he paints the animals and their world nowadays, he does it with a sense of urgency hoping people will come to value them as he does. Believing that the world of the sea mammal is particularly under threat he feels that books like this one can help to show how wonderful, irreplaceable and vulnerable it is.